Won-Buddhism:

The Birth of Korean Buddhism

Joon-sik Choi

Translated by Sandra Choe

Jimoondang
Seoul

Jimoondang
514-7 Munbal-ri, Gyoha-eup, Paju-si, Gyeonggi-do, 413-756, Korea
95 Waryong-dong, Jongno-gu, Seoul, 110-360, Korea
227 Suttons Lane, Edison, NJ 08817, USA
Phone: 82-2-743-0227 E-mail: edit@jimoon.co.kr
82-2-743-3192~3 E-mail: sale@jimoon.co.kr
Fax: 82-2-743-3097, 82-2-742-4657
Homepage: www.jimoon.co.kr

The National Library of Korea Cataloging-in-Publication (CIP)
Won-Buddhism: The Birth of Korean Buddhism
by Joon-sik Choi
Translated by Sandra Choe

Paju: Jimoondang, 2011
ISBN 978-89-6297-035-7 93220 228.95-KDC5 294.39-DDC21 CIP2011003231

Printed in Korea

Sot'aesan

Sot'aesan with his followers

Sot'aesan with Japanese officials

Il-Won-Sang made by female priests

Il-Won-Sang at the altar

Chŏngsan

Awakening Hall at Youngsan

various early canons of Won Buddhism

Wonkwang University

Acknowledgment

This book is presumably the first publication of the today that comprehensively covers Won Buddhism. Since Won Buddhism, one of the new religions of Korea, has devoted actively itself to missionary work, its scripture was translated into English early and it has been read by many people worldwide.

Even though the scripture for Won Buddhism is composed of simple content and translated in a concise and intelligible form, it is not easy to understand; it only conveys the essential teachings of Won Buddhism. Besides important teachings or philosophy, there are many interesting stories such as history and legend in Won Buddhism which are not contained in its scripture but worth being shared with readers. Thus I believed that the introductory book on Won Buddhism written in English is very necessary for the better understanding of Won Buddhism.

Around the time I met Minister (of Won Buddhism) Daesun Kim, the president of Wonlim Promotion Society and we both agreed about the need of the publication of a general introductory book on Won Buddhism. Especially I am very gratitude to Minister Kim for his financial assistance to this book which had to be translated into English. My greatest gratitude also goes to Jimoondang publishing company for their efforts to publish this book. Moreover, I owe special thanks to my former student, Sandra Choe who translated the entire text of this book. Lastly, I wish this book would bring some benefits to readers in English-speaking countries in order to understand Korean religions better.

Joon-sik Choi
in 2011

Preface

It must have been around March 1981. I had just arrived in the United States to begin my doctorate degree. Needing a place to stay, I contacted a high school classmate currently at the New York Won Buddhism Temple. There was a lot of time left until the semester began in September, and now that I was in America for the first time, I wanted to see New York City. Thus I headed to where my old classmate was living. I was fairly occupied during the day exploring downtown New York via metro, but there was nothing to do in the early morning and late at night. I was staying at the Won Buddhism Temple, where alcohol and television were not allowed.

It was then that my classmate suggested reading through *The Scriptures of Won Buddhism* (hereafter, *Scriptures*). Although I had come to the US to major in religion, at the time I knew very little about Won Buddhism. Embarrassingly enough, most other Koreans back then probably knew no more than I did. Upon flipping through the book, I noticed that it was entirely in Hangeul and thought that if nothing else, it would at least be an easy read.[1]

1 Hangeul is the name of the Korean alphabet. Compared to pictogram Chinese characters,

Without any prior knowledge or idea of what to expect, I began reading, believing that it would roughly resemble most other religious scriptures.

However, the more I read, I found myself astonished. To think that such an extraordinary individual had been with us until the very recent past! The character of Founding Master Sot'aesan that I met in the *Scriptures* was as grand and magnificent as a mountain range. His teachings not only accommodated all other teachings but were described very logically. I do not ordinarily read the same book twice, but I ended up reading the Scriptures twice in one sitting. I had thought that there were only independence fighters such as An Changho and Kim Gu who had illuminated the Japanese colonial period,[2] failing to realize that there had also been a great teacher in a remote corner of Chŏlla Province who dreamed of the Great Opening of Korea and the world.[3]

At this, people often jokingly reproach me, pointing out that "there is no way such a great teacher of faith could have come from an obscure little country like Korea." It is then my duty to insist that I do not say such things because of exaggerated nationalism or chauvinism. Having read my share of books on religion, ranging from the Ramakrishna and Ramana Maharishi to the modern sages, I always stress that Sot'aesan is no less great than these. But such observations are always met with little

---

as a phonetic alphabet it is much easier to read and write.

2 Korea was a colony of Japan from 1910 until 1945; this period is known as either the Japanese occupation or the Japanese colonial period. Various resistance movements took place throughout the colonial period, for which many independence fighters were incarcerated. An Changho is one of the most famous of these fighters; there is a highway bearing his name in Los Angeles.

3 South Korea is divided into eight provinces. The three that will be mentioned throughout this book are the furthest south on the peninsula: North and South Chŏlla Province (southest) and Kyŏngsang Province (southeast).

enthusiasm.

My complaint on this matter is a very simple one. Koreans, fully aware of the value of traditional culture, designate human cultural treasures and regularly custom-make the traditional attire known as *hanbok*. But why do they then ignore religious teachings that have been tailor-made specifically for Koreans? The teachings of indigenous Korean religions, beginning with Tonghak (Eastern Learning) and going up to Chŭngsangyo and Won Buddhism, are universal, but why do we so often ignore and even look down upon them? Great pains are taken to make sure that everything else in our lives is 'made in Korea,' but the truly important part —the mental component—is always sought from elsewhere.

I deeply regretted the fact that I had not been born earlier, to have met in person the great human being that was Sot'aesan. I would no doubt have asked to become his disciple. My classmate at the New York temple also admitted that he had not been proud of being Korean until he met Sot'aesan through Won Buddhism, after which he took boundless pride in having been born in the same country as the great leader.

Contents

Chapter 3

Chapter 4

Appendix

1

Chapter 1

A Mature and Enlightened Being

We will now meet Sot'aesan, an individual who resembles a formidable mountain ('san' means 'mountain' in Korean).[1] His actual name is Chungbin Park (1891—1943). Before we look at Sot'aesan the individual, it is absolutely essential to examine his family background. In order to fully understand great people, it is necessary to go through the small, gossipy anecdotes about their families and how they grew up. In this way, we can learn everything possible about the person.

Interestingly, Sot'aesan is not the offspring of a first wife. Sot'aesan's father, Sŏngsam Park, first married a woman whose surname was Lim and had two sons and one daughter.[2] Sot'aesan

1 Biographical information about Sot'aesan is mostly taken from the five-volume series *Wŏnpulkyo Ch'ogi Kyodansa* (Early Won Buddhist History) by Minister Yongduk Park.

2 Women in the strictly patriarchal Chosŏn dynasty did not have official first names. Instead, they were referred to only by their maiden surnames. All women regardless

is not among the children from this first marriage, but it is at this time that Sŏngsam Park settles in Killyong-ni (a village in South Chŏlla Province) where Sot'aesan will later be born. Park then took into his home a woman named Yu, a young widow living in Killyong-ni at the time. It is impossible to know solely from Won Buddhist records whether Yu was taken as a consort or married through some other means. But in any case, Park's first wife died suddenly in her twenties, after which he raises his second wife to the status of main wife. Sot'aesan is the son of this second wife. Apparently it is no easy task for a great teacher to come into the world; Sot'aesan was born after his father and mother had each separated from their previous spouses.

Sŏngsam Park had one daughter and two sons with Sot'aesan's mother: our Sot'aesan was the second son, a middle child with one elder sister and one younger brother. What then did Sot'aesan's father do for a living? According to surviving records, Sŏngsam Park appears to have been highly intelligent, mediating for the villagers whenever there was a dispute to be settled. Because of his industrious nature, Park eventually ended up managing the rice fields of a wealthy neighborhood landlord (3,200 tons of rice). Thus, we can deduce that the Park household did not struggle to make ends meet. In fact, with servants and oxen, they were relatively well-off compared to other farming families. It was into such an environment that Sot'aesan was born in 1891. When his third son began religious training in earnest, Sŏngsam Park supported him with everything he had. Those who found religions are rarely fortunate enough to receive full backing from their families, but Sot'aesan did. However, such fortune did not last

---

of social class usually did have first names, but this was only used by her immediate family before she was married.

long. Sŏngsam Park died abruptly in 1910, when twenty- year-old Sot'aesan was still in the middle of his training. It is said that Sot'aesan suffered immense damages because of his father's death, a point which I will return to in a later section.

Before we begin to investigate Sot'aesan's childhood and youth, let us first briefly look at stories about his siblings and children. Lay readers need not know all the details about Sot'aesan's family tree, but in order to understand Sot'aesan it is important to know what his blood relatives thought of him. Those who we regard as pillars of society are often evaluated completely differently by their families. Of course, this does not mean that those who are not respected by their families are not admirable people. However, if such an individual has the respect of his immediate family, this is usually not unfounded. Because family members live in very close quarters, everything about oneself ends up being revealed. Thus, if someone has the respect of the people he interacts with every day, there is a high probability that he is a mature individual whose actions match his words.

There is no doubt that Sot'aesan had the respect of his family. In general, we know that his stepbrothers actively supported his work, his sister eventually converted to Won Buddhism and her son entered the Won Buddhist order as a monk. Sot'aesan's eldest son (Kiljin Park) became the first president of Wonkwang University, a Won Buddhist institution, and his eldest daughter's son—this daughter is Sot'aesan's first child—was a Won Buddhist monk who also served as president of Wonkwang University. Sot'aesan's younger brother converted to the teachings of Won Buddhism and became one of his nine disciples. Many of the descendants of this younger brother have also converted to Won Buddhism or entered the priesthood. Not only have many of the great-grandchildren become followers but some of them are monks at the frontlines of evangelism work or are university professors.

I once met Sot'aesan's eldest son Kiljin Park when I visited Wonkwang University as an undergraduate. Even then I did not know anything about Won Buddhism and thus only knew him as the president of Wonkwang, but I still vividly remember his commanding presence. He did not exude the usual authoritative air of a university president. It was a passing meeting on the street, but I remember him telling me that "the best type of learning is to meet many great people and hear what they have to say." I firmly believe that I still recall this brief conversation from many years ago because he was that great of a man. If this is the son, what must the father have been like? It makes me regret not having been born several decades earlier. I say this because I also believe that the best way to learn is to have a great teacher. The combined knowledge of thousands of books does not measure up to one meeting with a teacher. That is how important the meeting of one individual with another is. Everyone who ever had contact with Sot'aesan probably had accumulated a veritable mountain of virtue in their previous lives. Zhaozhou (趙州), the greatest monk of the Tang dynasty, once declared that if anyone who comes to him does not become enlightened within three years, he would willingly die on the spot. That is the weight of a teacher-disciple relationship. This is why in Eastern countries like India and China, a teacher is considered more important than a parent. In my fifty years I still have not met anyone with an ideal personality. Within modern Korean history, we can perhaps say that An Changho was close to being an ideal personality. In an age that has not produced any great personalities, someone like Sot'aesan is sorely missed.

A Mature Childhood Full of Big Ideas

A Courageous Child

Many stories are told about Sot'aesan's childhood. Each time I read them, I receive the impression that Sot'aesan had a bold personality and was mature beyond his years. Let us first look at his unusual personality. There is a story of when he was about four or five years old that he chased away a serpent from which his friends all ran away. But much more noteworthy is the incident in which he scared his father. Sot'aesan is said to have been four years old. While eating his dinner, Sot'aesan decided that he wanted more rice. He then proceeded to take some rice from his father's bowl (Something like this never happened in a strictly patriarchal society). While thinking that it was cute of his young son, Sŏngsam decided that he could not let this incident pass and threatened to whip him. At this, Sot'aesan declared that if his father whipped him, he would give him a huge surprise. Sŏngsam laughed him off and forgot about the incident altogether. Several hours later, Sot'aesan yelled from the village entrance that rebellion army soldiers were coming. At the time, there were many wandering bandits who pretended to be in the rebellion army and plundered villages; the mere mention of rebellion army was enough to make people tremble with fear. Scared awake from his nap, Sot'aesan's father went into the bamboo forest in the backyard and stayed there for some time until he realized that Sot'aesan had lied. To think that a mere four-year-old could cause such a commotion! It would not have been easy for an adult to think of such an idea; that a small child not only thought of the idea himself but put it into action is beyond understanding.

There is a related story in which the village teacher was given a similar shock. This occurred when Sot'aesan was ten years old. Having promised to scare his teacher, who insisted that he had never been scared in his life, Sot'aesan set fire to the firewood at his teacher's house. Of course the teacher was frightened out of his mind. The very fact that such stories remain proves that Sot'aesan was no ordinary child. Becoming enlightenment actually requires a great deal of courage. Courage in this case is not a mobster breaking whiskey glasses with his teeth. According to the tales of mystics, once we go deep enough into our subconscious, we come face to face with an enormous negative energy. Some call this the devil, but it is probably the mind's creation of a negative image of ourselves. In an ordinary state, we are unable to face these inner demons, either because they are too gruesome or too evil. The late Mother Teresa also seems to have endured this hardship, having exorcised demons not only during her lifetime but also just before her death. For the reader's reference, a high degree of spirituality also implies a corresponding degree of diabolic energy. Although exorcism alone probably would not eliminate this energy, I have not heard anything more about Mother Teresa's experiences with this and thus cannot make any conclusive judgment. In any case, in order to confront these types of things one needs to be truly courageous. These stories about Sot'aesan prove that he had the potential to become enlightened from very early in his life. In other words, Sot'aesan already possessed the strength to fight his demons.

A Child who likes religious questions

One common feature of many religious sages is that they were awakened to fundamental religious questions from early childhood. One example is the shock that young Buddha received upon observing the cycle of a small insect, a larger insect and a bird eating and being eaten by each other. Jesus was no exception. The only story told about his childhood is of the twelve-year-old Jesus preaching in the Jewish synagogue, shocking all of his listeners. Jesus was an extremely precocious child! The Japanese Zen priest Dōgen entered the priesthood after watching smoke rise up from the cremation of his dead father's body and realizing the impermanence of human life. These anecdotes show how sensitive and mature religious sages are from an early age.

Sot'aesan is not found lacking in this respect. He began asking religious questions when he was seven years old. The first fundamental question he ever had was, interestingly enough, about natural phenomena. Sot'aesan wondered "how the sky was so high and blue and clean" as well as "how clouds and rain fall from such a clean sky." According to stories told about him, he always finished what he began. Thus, it is unlikely that these questions were asked and then immediately forgotten. It is said that he once climbed a mountain after noticing that it seemed to reach the sky; another time, he saw clouds perched on a mountain top and set off to climb the mountain, saying that he would catch the clouds.

However, it is noteworthy that the types of questions Sot'aesan asked as a child are different from those of past Buddhist sages. The typical sequence of events is that the sage will have a conversion experience after realizing the impermanence of life. This is in line with the Buddhist doctrine that all things are impermanent. In comparison, Sot'aesan's questions are difficult to contextualize because they are about the laws of nature rather than life's fundamental problems; people who ask these types of questions usually become scientists, whereas Sot'aesan became the founder of a religion.

When he is eleven years old, young Sot'aesan hears something from an older relative while the family is at the local mountain performing ancestral rites.[3] The tip was that any and all questions about life can be answered by the mountain spirit. Sot'aesan immediately decided to pray in order to meet the mountain spirit. The place where he prayed is a nearby mountain where tigers were rumored to appear. The way in which he prayed was not particularly special: after placing fruit and rice cakes on a boulder as an offering, he would bow in the four cardinal directions and fervently pray. According to the records, Sot'aesan prayed in this fashion for five years rain or shine without missing a single day. Although he did attend the village school, apparently Sot'aesan was not interested in book learning and only focused on his prayers. This type of perseverance and concentration is a necessity for people who are captivated by fundamental questions; Sot'aesan is not lacking in this regard. Let us think about that for a moment. Sot'aesan was around eleven or twelve years old when he began praying, the age that a child today begins middle school. To have been curious about these kinds of things so young, and the fact that he prayed at a rather dangerous site for four years seems

3 Ancestor worship does not literally mean the worship of one's ancestors as if they are gods. Instead, it is an elaborate ritual which honors the memory of the family's past four patriarchs and takes place either at home or at the family burial grounds. Although ancestor worship was practiced in previous dynasties as well, it became particularly important (and male-centric) during the Chosŏn dynasty (1392—1910), the last period of dynastic rule before the colonial period. It is still a common practice today.

rather extreme even for a sage.

Of course, Sot'aesan did not only pray during this time. He was married at fifteen, but this did not put an end to his prayers; Sot'aesan continued going to the mountain for another year after getting married. Then one day during his fifth year of prayer, he realized that his quest for the mountain spirit was useless. After having shown such devotion, the mountain spirit's silence caused him to doubt the spirit's very existence. There is an amusing anecdote about the last day of prayer. It is said that several hundred monks came down the mountain, singing and dancing and generally causing a great commotion, and then suddenly disappeared. Whether this was a hallucination or an actual event we cannot know.

After putting an end to his prayers, Sot'aesan still had gnawing doubts. When he was sixteen years old and at his wife's family home for lunar New Year, he overheard someone reading aloud the classical novel *Tale of Choung*. Set in the Song dynasty, this didactic novel is basically about a man named Choung who, with the help of a man with unusual abilities, takes revenge for his father's death and rescues the crumbling Song regime from complete destruction. Although the synopsis itself is uninspiring, it must not have seemed so to Sot'aesan. He had an epiphany in which he decided that "finding a man with extraordinary abilities will answer all of my questions." In retrospect this may seem rather naïve, but for Sot'aesan, who had been latched onto these doubts night and day, it was a major breakthrough. It is through such repeated trial and error, rather than a one-time stroke of luck, that anyone achieves anything of value. It is better to succeed at least once after ten tries than not achieve anything at all because of a fear of failure.

The Road to Truth

In Search of a Teacher

At this time Sot'aesan had just turned sixteen. For the next five years, he searched far and wide for an extraordinary man to be his teacher. Whenever he saw someone who seemed even slightly unusual, he either went to see him or spared no pains to invite the person to his own home, all in hopes of learning what he seeked. But most of these encounters ended in failure and he was unable to meet the hoped-for extraordinary man. To assist the reader's understanding of the situation, let us consider one example. Sot'aesan calls to his home a person—it appears that he at times sought out beggars solely because of their shabby appearance—who is supposedly an eccentric. The 'eccentric' declares that he can control powerful spirits and that if Sot'aesan wants to learn this ability, he must first pay one ox. Sot'aesan replies that if the eccentric can first show him a spirit, he will provide the ox. At this, the eccentric tries to call upon the spirits by chanting spells for several days and nights; unfortunately, no spirit appears. The eccentric then escapes in the middle of the night.

An event occurs around this time that I feel compelled to share. Sot'aesan visited a Buddhist temple, where the monks were worshipping before a life-size Buddha statue as if it were a living being. Sot'aesan, unable to bypass anything without first testing it out, decided to test the Buddha statue to see why people were worshipping it. Sot'aesan embarks on a dangerous and earnest but also highly amusing experiment: he decides to desecrate the Buddha statue. With the strange conviction that if the 'idol' did have power it would punish him, he slapped its face and punched its waist. While he was no ordinary individual, Sot'aesan apparently feared that there would be retribution. After a night spent quaking in fear, he awoke the next morning to find that nothing had happened. Sot'aesan concluded that "had the statue truly had power, it would have punished me for what I did. Even if it did not out of compassion, should it not have at least chastised me in my dreams? All idols are just superstition." In a sense the logic seems too simplistic, while on the other hand it gives us valuable insight into the scrupulous mind that went to such lengths to physically experiment something so easy to prove. It is a strange incident that is difficult to evaluate with one single perspective. Won Buddhists worship without a Buddha statue; instead, there is only a large circle on the wall. This revolutionary approach to 'idol' elimination is most likely the result of Sot'aesan's aforementioned experience.

Sot'aesan's experiences with different religions did not end with Buddhism. There was no chance of foregoing Christianity, which by that time had already begun making significant inroads into Korea. After attending a local church service and hearing that only God decides whether a person is wealthy or poor, the length of his life and whether or not he is fortunate, Sot'aesan decided to conduct an experiment on the heavens. Upon returning home, Sot'aesan did something strange. Shaking a stick at the sky, he apparently shouted, "You up there! If you truly have miraculous powers, show a sign. If you do not, stay as you are!" Although he was nervous about it, there was no reaction from the sky. Sot'aesan concluded that whether made into an image or not, all 'idols' are worthless and do not provide any answers.

All things begin with something simple. It is only after one thoroughly analyzes such simple things that it is then possible to answer the bigger questions. There are various moments in history in which someone with pure intentions challenged a system that had been taken for granted, thus exposing its faults. There are those who may object that questioning religion is not the proper attitude to have toward faith. While this may sound reasonable, it can actually be a very dangerous philosophy. We cannot unconditionally accept faith, something more precious than life itself, without any thought. Because it is so precious, it must constantly be questioned and tested. Faith is something that is unshakeable under any circumstances. Accepting the church's demand that the grace of God is only for those who believe unconditionally without any objections can be rash. Within this context, the various experiments of Sot'aesan that we have just seen look even more remarkable.

While having these fundamental questions, Sot'aesan suffers two large setbacks: the collapse of his country and the death of his father. After the death of his father, who had been responsible for the family's livelihood, Sot'aesan pauses his search for truth and turns his attention to worldly matters. The family had basic needs to be met as well as accumulated debts to be paid. Sot'aesan tried running a tavern and selling goods at the marketplace. But neither endeavor seems to have been successful: religious training has little to do with business acumen. By going into business at the Pŏpsŏngpo fish market, he unexpectedly earned some money and was able to pay off the debts. This fish market is a market at which fishermen give their catch (from the Yellow Sea) to a middleman, who then gives them food and other basic essentials and hands over the fish to merchants on land.

The story of Sot'aesan calming the sea is treated as a legend within the Won Buddhist order. The boat carrying Sot'aesan's group suddenly met with heavy wind and waves, rendering absolute chaos on board. Everyone on the boat was terrified, and even the ferryman, at a complete loss, was sobbing in a corner. Sot'aesan slapped the ferryman across the face several times and severely chastised him, "If you lose your head now, even those who could have lived will die. We're all about to die. Don't lose your head." He then turned to the sky. "Gods of heaven and earth! Innocent people are about to die because of my sins. If you are going to send punishment, punish only me." After shouting this two or three times, the waves died down as if nothing had happened.

Stories like this one also appear in the scriptures of other religions. The most similar example is the story of Jesus having calmed the storm at sea. These stories are probably told in order to prove that the founder of the religion had extraordinary powers that could control even nature. Thus, regardless of their veracity, there is a natural tendency for them to be told amongst the disciples. In the case of Sot'aesan, there is no way of knowing whether or how much these stories have been dramatized or not. What we can see is the extent to which the disciples viewed their teacher as an extraordinary figure.

'What am I to do?'

After having paid all the debts, it was time to return to the search for truth. From this point until the moment of enlightenment, control over oneself is lost: all that is done is sitting, staring vacantly and worrying. The *koan* that Sot'aesan latched onto during this time was 'what am I to do?,' which refers to the many unanswered questions that had been piling up since childhood.[4]

Ordinary laypeople who are not interested in things like this may wonder why it is so important, but for religious individuals there is nothing of greater importance. Indeed, what is more important than becoming enlightened and knowing the fundamental meaning of life? Paul Tillich, the greatest theologian of the twentieth century, defined religious faith as the state in which one is grasped by ultimate concern. Once one is caught up in this, all other affairs of the world look minor in comparison. Sot'aesan's questions are reminiscent of the classic *koan* of Zen Buddhism: 'what is this?' This *koan* means 'what is my true self,' or more simply, 'who am I;' although this question is slightly different in terms of direction than that of Sot'aesan, it can be seen within the same general context.

While struggling with this *koan*, if he suddenly thought up a spell, Sot'aesan tried repeating it continuously without end. But most of his deepest concentration was on the question of 'what am I to do.' There are various stories that tell of the extent of Sot'aesan's concentration during this period. There were countless times that he would stop eating his meal and hold his spoon in the air. This means that he had fallen into a trance while eating. Because he was still for such long periods of time, it is said that swarms of flies would cling to him and suck up his rice and side dishes. Another story tells of how Sot'aesan forgot while he was in the bathroom and spent an entire afternoon standing there with his pants down. On rare occasions when his mind cleared, he would say that he was going to the market and then enter a trance while walking along the road with the merchants. He stood at the ferry for the whole day. The merchants, returning home in the

4 A *koan* is a nonsensical story that is used by Zen Buddhists to concentrate during meditation.

evening, found Sot'aesan still standing where they had left him. The small house where he meditated became rotten beyond repair; the front yard was full of weeds, and rainwater seeped into the floor. A boy who saw Sot'aesan at this stage described him in the following way: "His hair is wild and unkempt because it is not combed. He has forgotten to eat and sleep, and sits in one spot like a rice sack without moving." When he was not sitting in his room, there were times that he would stay up the entire night in the mountains, go into icy water or spend the entire night awake in a cold room. Sot'aesan had entered the stage in which all conscious feeling was gone.

Why do people who practice asceticism go into such deep trances? In other words, why must they concentrate so deeply? While the answer to this question is highly important, it is not the main subject of this book and thus I will not describe it at length. To present a summarized version, the focal point of meditation is concentration. Countless ascetics have invented various methods of meditation, but it eventually all boils down to how to concentrate effectively. Then why must one concentrate? True concentration means shutting off the left brain, the source of all kinds of knowledge and miscellaneous thoughts. The right brain controls wisdom, but it does not have much opportunity to act when the left brain is highly developed. Once the left brain, which sees everything through a logical and analytical lens, is turned off, the door to wisdom is flung wide open. Concentration paralyzes the brain's analytical function. Apart from this, concentration also shatters accumulated preconceptions and prejudices. But a discussion of these will become even more complicated. Let us move on from this point for now.

As can be predicted, the practice of such meditation day and night ravaged Sot'aesan's health. Moreover, practices like breath meditation, when done incorrectly, can cause serious illness. A practitioner doing everything on his own without a teacher is even more likely to become ill. According to folklore, Sot'aesan's stomach was grotesquely distended—filled with pus—as if a water jar had been placed inside it, his hair looked like a crow's nest and his body was covered with tumors and boil scabs. He was unable to stop coughing and was reduced to skin and bones from malnutrition. Villagers refused to go anywhere near Sot'aesan, believing that he had leprosy. Sot'aesan of course must have suffered greatly, but the same could be said for his wife and those close to him. The scriptures do not mention the people closest to him, but would they not have suffered as much if not more so than he? How difficult must this entire experience have been for his wife, whose husband had become like a leper from meditating all the time? Sot'aesan's wife in fact prayed at a spring for several years, while a woman called Paraenginae who often waited on Sot'aesan performed ablutions every morning and evening for his success.

It is said that various miracles took place near Sot'aesan at this time, but I will avoid all mention of these. Sot'aesan later declares that such miracles are as useless as a light bulb in the daytime and does not given them any significance. As the years passed and Sot'aesan turned twenty-five, he went even deeper into trance. He later told an interesting story about his state of mind during that time. It seems that he fluctuated between owning the entire universe and being unable to control his own body. Because this is such an interesting story, let us look at the Scripture itself:

The Founding Master said, "Before I gained my first thought of

> awakening, I sometimes offered up formal prayer, or recited spells that spontaneously arose in my mind, or fell unawares into a tranquil silence. After I inadvertently gained my first insight and the awakened perception cleared and the numinous gate sprang open, there continued to be fluctuations from brightness to darkness between one day's morning and evening, or between one month's two halves. During these fluctuations, when the gate of wisdom opened, I felt as if there were nothing under heaven I could not know or do; but when the gate closed again, I didn't have the faintest idea what to do with my own body and worried anew about my road ahead, even doubting whether I might not be possessed by some spirits. Eventually, however, those fluctuations disappeared, and my awakened perception continued consistently.
>
> • *The Scripture of the Founding Master*, Practice, 46 •

There is an interesting point in Sot'aesan's words. We may think that enlightenment is attained just once and that state continues for a lifetime, but Sot'aesan shows that this is not always the case. It is different from the sudden, instantaneous moment of enlightenment that is particularly emphasized by Zen Buddhism. I personally feel that the experience of Sot'aesan is more relatable. The approach of Zen Buddhism may look more 'spiritual,' but is it not true that life does not always happen so beautifully? Do people not fall down twelve times in a single day, but move on nonetheless? Is it not true that at times one feels that everything is going well and at other times that nothing will go well, and things are accomplished through a constant repetition of these two extremes?

Another noteworthy characteristic of Sot'aesan's mental training is that he did not leave home in order to seek truth. This is an extremely rare occurrence in human religious history. Almost all of those who founded large religions left the everyday realm of the home and went into the mountains or desert to meditate. This is most likely because what they were trying to achieve seemed impossible under ordinary circumstances. Even plain common sense dictates that one must be in an empty place to wrestle with Absolute Nothingness; attempting to achieve this task in a house filled with family would be a waste of time. Sot'aesan is extremely unique in that he went through none of these. This was perhaps a foreshadowing of the policy allowing marriage for the clergy in Won Buddhism.

One more interesting feature of Sot'aesan's training is that he became enlightened without the help of a teacher. But this is also true of many other great religious leaders and is not exclusive to Sot'aesan. Nevertheless, it is not a common occurrence.

Reaching Enlightenment

Sot'aesan was getting closer to enlightenment; the closer he got, the sicker he became. He suffered from severe cold and fever, his stomach was swollen outward as far as it could stretch, and his entire body excluding the face was so thickly covered with boils that scabs needed to be removed by the bucketful every day. At their wit's end, Sot'aesan's family visited fortune tellers and even conducted shamanic rites. Considering all the myriad difficulties involved in the process, there is relatively little written about the moment that Sot'aesan actually becomes enlightened. Generally, the story goes that wisdom came upon him at dawn on April 28, 1916. He then composed aloud a poem: "When a fresh wind blows and the moon rises, all things become bright." On the other hand, early Won Buddhist records show that Sot'aesan resolved all of his former doubts and became enlightened that day upon hearing the scriptures of Tonghak (Korean new religion) and *Book of Change*[5] being read aloud.

Regardless of how he became enlightened, there is one doubtful point. Most stories about the founders of major religions are sure to include a tale about the last battle with the devil just before reaching enlightenment or receiving the Holy Spirit. Buddha is tempted three times by evil spirits the night before he becomes enlightened, and Jesus is also said to be tempted three times by the devil in the desert. Not only these two but all other saint and holy figures go through the same experience, thus coining the term 'dark night of the soul.' It is the last fight against the remaining negative energy in the deepest parts of the heart. But this type of experience is not mentioned in the records on Sot'aesan. I am not sure how this should be understood, or whether it is possible to achieve enlightenment without going through a last test.

Nevertheless, the first thing that Sot'aesan did after becoming enlightened was to tidy his appearance. As previously mentioned, Sot'aesan's health was put under severe strain during his training. His first act was to look for a comb to brush his hair, scissors to cut his nails and a basin of water to wash his face. After becoming whole again, Sot'aesan wanted to test himself to see whether he had truly become enlightened or whether he merely under an illusion. Because he had become enlightened without a teacher, it is natural that he wanted some type of recognition. Thus, the first books that he sought out were ones that were relatively easy to obtain: *Sohak* and Four Books, both Confucian classics. *Sohak* is a textbook for children that teaches the Confu-

---

5 What Sot'aesan is said to have heard is the following: "One who is great, together with heaven and earth, is virtuous, shines with the sun and moon as one, follows the order of the four seasons, and rules over prosperity and disaster with the spirits."

cian ethics. In addition to these, he also read the major scriptures of Tonghak, the Taoist scriptures *Ŭmpukyŏng* and *Okch'ukyŏng*, and the Christian Bible. Upon reading all of these books, Sot'aesan realized that his enlightenment had already been accomplished. However, it is said that he was unable to agree fully with any of the aforementioned scriptures. Strangely enough, it was the following year that Sot'aesan obtained Buddhist scriptures. After reading the *Diamond Sutra*, which was obtained from the nearby Pulgap Temple, Sot'aesan realized that his teachings completely overlapped with Buddhist teachings. According to him, Buddha is a saint among saints and there are many similarities between himself and Buddha, including the reason for enlightenment and how he was saved. At this time, Sot'aesan decided to base his teachings on Buddhism, or "trace the origins to Buddhism" in Won Buddhist terminology.

However, early Won Buddhist history shows that Won Buddhism began differently. Sot'aesan was rather lonely after becoming enlightened. Having been treated as dead for years, this seems to be a natural reaction. Villagers would not have been quick to acknowledge the enlightened status of someone they had ostracized. Moreover, there were few educated people in Sot'aesan's community, and thus most were more easily convinced by displays of supernatural power than religious doctrine. Nevertheless, one could not simply bemoan fate. Sot'aesan decided to perform rituals in the style of Chŭngsangyo, a popular religion of the day. It is said that if one chants the T'aeŭlchu, the most famous spell of Chŭngsangyo, and performs a ritual, one can communicate with the spirits as well as heal illnesses and perform supernatural feats. People living in Chŏlla Province at the time seemed to have strong faith in this religion. Sot'aesan must have planned to strengthen his own basis by performing this ritual; after seven days of this, Sot'aesan declared that he had become spiritually awakened. Overseeing this ritual were Sot'aesan's sworn elder brother Sŏngsŏp Kim (an avid believer of Chŭngsangyo) and Sŏngkuk Yu, Sot'aesan's maternal uncle and a believer of Tonghak. Sŏngsŏp Kim was twelve years older than Sot'aesan and Sŏngkuk Yu was Sot'aesan's uncle, but both became key disciples. The relationship between teacher and disciple was determined not by seniority in age or kinship ties but solely by understanding of the Buddhist teaching. In this regard, I evaluate Sot'aesan highly. Not having been anywhere near enlightenment myself, I cannot tell whether or not Sot'aesan was enlightened; I can only conjecture with circumstantial evidence. The fact that Sot'aesan's relatives converted shows that his enlightenment was not merely an illusion. While it is easy to fool strangers, it is difficult to fool those who are close to us. Even so, is it not said that prophets are unwelcome in their own hometowns?

In any case, after Sot'aesan openly declares that he has 'opened his eyes,' people began to gather to him. Within four months, nearly 40 people had gathered, showing that the rituals must have had some effect. This seems more believable than the story we looked at just earlier about Sot'aesan deciding to establish his roots in Buddhism after reading the *Diamond Sutra.* The story about the *Diamond Sutra* is said to have been told in order to escape the long arm of the Japanese colonial government, which was strongly opposed to indigenous religions. In other words, the order invented the story about Buddhism to avoid persecution by the Japanese, who cracked down harshly on all indigenous religions except Buddhism.

Sot'aesan's First Dharma[6]

Corresponding Lifegiving of the Strong and the Weak

While it is unclear whether these dharma words were given to his newly acquired disciples or were from an earlier occasion, Sot'aesan gives his first dharma talk (Buddhist sermon) after becoming enlightened. He discusses several different concepts, but the unifying theme is the way the weak become the strong. The main idea of this sermon is the corresponding lifegiving between the strong and the weak. It is easy to see why Sot'aesan gave this sermon as his first dharma talk; Korea at the time was a Japanese colony. Unbecoming of someone enlightened within the Buddhist tradition, Sot'aesan remained interested in social issues. We will see this more clearly later, but the importance of a proper society is mentioned numerous times throughout his teachings.

It was the first of many dharma talks: let us observe a few of its characteristics before moving on. It is the natural way of the world that there are those who are weak and those who are strong; in order to achieve peace, they must find a way of coexisting. Sot'aesan first admonishes the strong. There is no such thing in the world as one who is eternally strong. He theorizes that if the strong desire to remain strong, they must pull up the weak to the level of the strong. If this does not occur and the strong exploit the weak with their strength, the former will eventually fall to the level of the latter. On the other hand, if the

6 After Buddha became enlightened in northern India, he gave a sermon to five disciples with whom he had undergone ascetic practice. The sermon was about the Four Noble Truths which became the most basic doctrine of Buddhism. This was Buddha's first dharma.

weak do not think to train their abilities so that they can rise to the position of the strong and only fight amongst themselves and blame only the strong, they will never shake free from the fetters of the weak. The message illustrated here is a fairly generic one, but prompts a great deal of thought. The strong tend to be arrogant, but the law of the world dictates that there is always a counteraction for each strength. Thus, there is always an energy that works against the arrogance of the strong. When these two collide, the strong receive a huge shock. However, if the strong show compassion for the weak, they will be able to maintain their position.

Selecting the Core Disciples

As more people gathered around Sot'aesan, he quickly began to form an organization. The system that he created was a 'ten person, one unit' format. One unit consisted of ten people, and each person in this unit would in turn create another unit of ten, resulting in a pyramidal organization. Sot'aesan stated that in a unit, the unit leader was the sky, the central member the earth, and the remaining eight unit members were the eight trigrams (as used in *The Book of Changes*). Expounding upon the superiority of this arrangement, Sot'aesan reasoned that it was a very handy system because only one person was needed to teach hundreds of millions of others and thus only needed to be concerned with teaching nine. He is in fact correct. Do not all things work this way? No matter how large of an organization or how great the task accomplished, all such groups begin with just a handful of like-minded people. Sot'aesan was already fully aware that the first step is the most important one.

Sot'aesan eventually chooses eight disciples. But why eight instead of nine? Sot'aesan's answer was that the central position was left empty because his primary disciple had not yet arrived. Sot'aesan's successor Chŏngsan appears two years later and becomes the greatest disciple. We will look at this more carefully later. The other eight disciples were also interesting figures. Firstly, most of them are from Sot'aesan's immediate surroundings. The majority either grew up with Sot'aesan or was introduced to him by those who did. Many were also older. We saw earlier that Sŏngsŏp Kim and Sŏngkuk Yu (twelve and eleven years older than Sot'aesan, respectively) became Sot'aesan's disciples without regard for age or kinship rank. There was even a disciple who was eighteen years older. Sot'aesan's younger brother also entered this group. In terms of religious affiliation, over half were not only well-versed in the Chinese classics but had also entered either Chŭngsangyo or Tonghak.

Looking over records on the disciples reminds me of several things. Firstly, I mentioned briefly before that Sot'aesan followed a highly unconventional procedure. Not only did he train without leaving home but his disciples were all people from his immediate environment. It is said that the Way is a return to normalcy: Sot'aesan fully embodied this tenet. He did not choose a special environment or work with unique people; instead, he accomplished an extremely difficult feat in a very ordinary environment. Winning over those who are closest to you is a difficult task. In Korean society, it is even more difficult if those people are also older. Amidst a social atmosphere in which fights frequently broke out because of disputes over who is higher or lower in age or seniority, the fact that these people disregarded all trappings of age and kinship rank in order to become disciples of Sot'aesan implies a great deal. This shows that either Sot'aesan was extraordinarily charismatic or that the extent of his enlightenment was truly astonishing.

The other interesting facet is the religious atmosphere of the Korean countryside at the time. As we have seen thus far, over half of Sot'aesan's disciples were former followers of Tonghak or Chŭngsangyo. Is this not strange? How was it that people were so devoted to religion—most people lived from hand to mouth—when times were so hard? If this situation defies understanding, let us consider rural Korea today. How many farmers would there be who were devoted to prayer and Taoist magic? Would not most people be hard-pressed just to eke out a living? But during a time when extreme poverty was the norm, people trained the mind in a leisurely manner. How can this be explained? Was this phenomenon unique to the hamlets near Sot'aesan's village? Or was this common throughout the peninsula? Moreover, we can assume that the influence of Tonghak and Chŭngsangyo was considerable. The fact that such religions had followers even in a remote village like Sot'aesan's hometown—today there are almost no believers of Tonghak or Chŭngsangyo in these villages!—is indicative of the large support base that Korean folk religions enjoyed at the time. How has this now changed? There is now no rural village that does not have its own church; this means that Christianity has now filled in that space.

Chapter 2

Into the World

The Beginning of a Savings Cooperative

Sot'aesan was a unique religious teacher, to say the least. Most cease to care about worldly matters after they become enlightened or have a major religious experience, but this was not the case with Sot'aesan. Plenty of evidence points to the fact that Sot'aesan cared deeply about the layout of his organization. Through this organization, he tried to rebuild society as Koreans knew it at the time. The first thing that Sot'aesan did with his disciples was not the creation of a religious training community but something much closer to a savings cooperative. He advised his disciples to begin saving up money, emphasizing the need for stable finances in order to train properly. Because the nature of saving requires that money not be spent, Sot'aesan instructed his disciples to stop purchasing cigarettes and alcohol and to instead save up small quantities of rice. Sot'aesan also employed more proactive methods of saving money: starting his own business. The industry that Sot'aesan chose to enter is what we today call distribution and shipping. He would buy up charcoal and resell it when market prices for charcoal had skyrocketed; this sometimes brought in as much as a 1,000% profit margin.

Once some money had been accumulated, Sot'aesan did something even more bizarre. It was the famous levee construction project, one of the most important events in Won Buddhist history.[1] Why did Sot'aesan insist on going through with the land reclamation project, something that has little to do with religious work? Various questions come to mind, but in early days of Won Buddhism, the levee project was probably second in importance only to Sot'aesan becoming enlightened. With his disciples, Sot'aesan succeeds in converting approximately 24 acres of mud flat near his hometown into rice fields. As with any project of this scale, there were various obstacles to be overcome by the group, including fund shortages as well as ridicule from the community. The most serious of these was probably the incident in which they almost lost the mud flat to someone else. One wealthy individual, tempted by the sudden 'availability' of a large field plot, tried to extort reclamation rights. The disciples were outraged by this close call. Sot'aesan countered that "even if the fruits of our exertion were to end up as [the rich man's] possession," there was nothing to fear. He reminded his disciples of the original purpose of the levee project, which was to help the greater public. Because the

1 In November 1918 Sot'aesan established an office to oversee the levee project. It was given an unusual name that consisted of a long string of Chinese characters. Perhaps it was considered too long; the name was later changed to Buddhist Dharma Society (Pulpŏb Yŏnguhoe).

man who had attempted to take the land is technically part of that greater public, Sot'aesan reasoned that the Won Buddhist community would still have ended up being the beneficiary of the whole thing.

This type of reaction shows that Sot'aesan was an unusually tolerant person. It shows that he refused to be restricted by (what he sees to be) inconsequential matters and, moreover, that he overcame the dictates of the ego. In psychology, the definition of a mature personality is someone for whom the group is a higher priority than oneself. On the other hand, a small-minded person evaluates all situations by the degree to which he or she will benefit from it. But someone with a mature personality takes a bird's eye view of the situation and works for the benefit of the group. There is another famous incident which illustrates this aspect of Sot'aesan's nature. One day while out walking with his disciples, he found an aged pine tree.[2] One disciple remarked that it would look lovely planted in front of their temple. Sot'aesan harshly rebuked what he considered to be the disciple's lack of thought; if the pine tree and the temple are both within the same fence, what need is there to replant the tree? In other words, Sot'aesan was saying that our backyard is the entire world, a very broad-minded principle. Is this not befitting of an enlightened being?

However, this begs the question why Sot'aesan began the levee project in the first place. The arduous training alone would have attracted people to him in droves. Instead, Sot'aesan started a long-term construction project. We have seen so many false prophets in our midst—those who, once they are recognized as

---

2 One of the ten symbols of longevity, pine trees were highly valuable during the Chosŏn dynasty. Ones with trunks bent by age and branches that grew close to the ground were especially valued.

'prophets' put on all sorts of airs. But Sot'aesan was different: his heart was set on the creation of a strong organization, for which the foundations must be firmly in place. It was probably to achieve this that Sot'aesan undertook the levee project. In this type of organization, the most important factor is solidarity. Moreover, there needs to be a strong underlying reserve of power that can be relied upon to get through all sorts of problems, a power which can only be strengthened by setting a goal and working toward its achievement. In the process of achieving this goal, one would have to independently solve any and all problems that arise. Also, this enables members of an organization to cultivate a strong sense of community. Once the organization becomes confident of its abilities, it becomes virtually undefeatable. Sot'aesan once said that he had begun various religious works in his previous lives, but that this one was the biggest of them all. He prophesized that although he was in a forgotten rural backwater, eventually the entire world would come to know about Won Buddhism. In hindsight, his prophesy has been more or less fulfilled. Although like all other religions it has its share of problems, it is undeniable Won Buddhism is spreading throughout the world.

Spiritual motive was not the only factor behind the construction plans. All work required financial backing to be accomplished. Because human beings have physical bodies, we must engage in economic activity to survive. Sot'aesan was well aware of this fact. One of the major doctrines of Won Buddhism is the Wholeness of both Spirit and Flesh (*yŏngyuk ssangchŏn*), meaning that mind and body coexist in perfection. The levee project is the best representation of this doctrine. Sot'aesan believed that in order to properly execute religious works, profit-oriented work should not be condemned as base but be further emphasized. It is possible for people to use profit-making work as a medium for spiritual growth in addition to the making of profit. What other way is there to achieve one's dreams other than through hard work? In this context, Sot'aesan's levee project brings to mind the teaching of a virtuous Zen master in the Tang dynasty: "If work is not done for one day, do not eat that day." For this master, manual labor and meditation were not separate entities. As can be seen here, Sot'aesan's teachings are always centered on the principle of all-encompassment; he did not exclude anything from his frame of reference. This is another 'trademark' of mature personalities.

Spiritual Consolidation

The Hearse of the Great Awakening: March First Movement

As the levee project was getting underway, the shadow of a gathering storm swept over the Korean peninsula: the March first movement. Because of allegations that the levee project may be connected to the March first movement, Sot'aesan was forced to undergo questioning for a week at the local precinct. This de facto arrest was the first of many times that Sot'aesan would be harassed by the Japanese colonial authorities. When the March first movement first broke out, Sot'aesan took a rather unexpected position on this nationwide uprising. The disciples must have been swept up by the excitement of the entire country rising up in the name of independence. However, Sot'aesan's response was that if his goal was the independence of Chosŏn, then he would of course participate in the movement. But because his goal was the salvation of the entire world, it would be best to remain uninvolved.

How should this be interpreted? We cannot know for sure whether Sot'aesan decided not to participate because of the above logic or fear that his newly begun organization might become jeopardized. Based on what we can glean from surviving records about his personality, this was clearly a difficult decision. By throwing himself and his organization into the March first movement, there was a big chance that he would be of little help to the movement and expose the group to danger. Moreover, his goal was much larger in scale. It may have been the case that with all of humanity to worry about saving, he could not allow himself to focus only on the independence of Chosŏn. Therefore, we cannot conclude that Sot'aesan's decision to not participate was a cowardly act. On the other hand, he did not underestimate the March first movement itself. He left the following comment about the movement: "The March first movement is the sound of the hearse urging on the Great Opening of a new world. We have so much to do now. Let us hurry and finish the levee project so that we may pray." I do not know why he compared the well-intentioned March first movement to a hearse. In any case, while the entire country threw itself against the Japanese as a human bullet, Sot'aesan and his disciples engaged in prayer, the highest type of mental activity. Won Buddhists regard the activity of this time as having been highly important.

Prayer of the Blood Stamp on White Paper

After the levee project, Sot'aesan felt that it was time to reign in the disciples' scattered thoughts and gave them another difficult task. Because a great deal of mental endurance would be required in order to deliver all sentient beings in the world, it would be necessary to pray to the heavens. This was the beginning of the hundred days' prayer. Sot'aesan ordered his core nine disciples to each go to a local mountain and pray three times per month for one hour each time. To ensure that the disciples would pray for one hour, Sot'aesan purchased nine pocket watches, an extremely valuable item at the time. The prayers went as planned. However, praying three times per month for one hour each is not extraordinary by any standard. Had the hundred days' prayers ended with this, it would not have been worth recording.

On the last day of the hundred days' prayer, Sot'aesan presented the disciples with a strange proposition. Although the prayers had been done well, it was insufficient because there were still lingering misgivings and doubts. Things up to this point are understandable, but Sot'aesan's next demand of his disciples is incomprehensible. He declared that they should all prove their determination to the gods of heaven and earth through death. Then the gods would be deeply moved and the true dharma of morality would be realized, bringing about a utopian age. Sot'aesan further incited his disciples, saying that they would be "honored as the saviors of the people." He added that anyone who did not want to sacrifice his life need not follow along. Perhaps because Sot'aesan's words were so earnest, the disciples decided that they would all die for the cause. Sot'aesan decided that the group would pray for ten more days and then die on the last day.

The last day of prayer finally dawned. It was the night of August 21, 1919. Everyone gathered in the office, each equipped with a newly sharpened dagger. Sot'aesan sat the disciples each according to his respective direction,—Chŏngsan was seated in the middle and the remaining eight were positioned according to the eight trigrams in the *Book of Change*—placed a bowl of clean water in the middle and then placed a watch and dagger in front of each disciple. He then calmly asked whether they would die without regret. To leave visible proof of such determination, he passed around a sheet of white paper onto which each person was to put his fingerprint. The disciples silently did as they were told without realizing how symbolic this act would end up becoming. Sot'aesan inspected the paper after everyone had finished, and said, "Good. There is a blood stamp." A blood stamp? What did he mean? Even though the fingerprints had been marked without any ink, their thumbprints on the paper "had turned as red as blood." Sot'aesan was greatly pleased, declaring that the group had finally been acknowledged by the gods.

He then said, "The deeds of the other world have been judged here today. We have succeeded." But what does this 'other world' refer to? Broadly speaking, the other world refers to a spiritual world beyond the one that we currently live in. According to the teachings of those who have undergone extensive mental training, everything that happens in this world occurs after it has first been decided in the other world. This is especially true of large-scale deeds. Sot'aesan is saying that his work has already been determined in the other world; in other words, it is finished. This is no easy task because receiving permission in the other world requires intense prayer and strong willpower. Sot'aesan had led his disciples up to this point in order to confirm their state of mind.

Sot'aesan is now feeling more at ease, but he does not let this on to the disciples. A few of them questioned the need to die if permission from the other world had already been given, but at this Sot'aesan smiled and commanded everyone to return to their places of prayer. In other words, everyone was to go to the mountains to die. Impossible to go against a teacher's demand, the disciples headed to their respective prayer places with dagger and pocket watch in tow. Upon hearing Sot'aesan call them back, the disciples turned around and returned to the spot they had departed from. Now that the gods of heaven and earth had been pleased and permission had been received from the other world, Sot'aesan told his disciples that now there was no need to die and they should live the rest of their lives in this same spirit. But it seems that the disciples had become overly excited by the night's events; Sot'aesan sent them back to the mountains to pray. After they returned, Sot'aesan gave each disciple a new name to mark the beginning of their new lives. Chŏngsan (in Korean, 'chŏng' means 'pot' and 'san' means 'mountain') is the name that was given at this time. The rest of the disciples were each named Ilsan ('mountain one'), Yisan ('mountain two') and so on until Palsan ('mountain eight'). I believe that this blood stamp prayer was the true starting point of the Won Buddhist faith. It was through this incident that the early spirit of Won Buddhism was fortified to the point of no return.

The question of how to interpret this prayer ceremony remains. In some ways it is an incident of colossal significance, while on the other hand it seems to be a performance that was tacitly agreed upon in advance. Several questions come to mind. After the disciples had earnestly prayed, Sot'aesan promised them that a morally righteous world would come if they committed joint suicide. But is this true? Would this world truly have been set right by the death of a few well-intentioned ascetics? It is difficult to make the world even a slightly better place after a lifetime of effort; what would have been the use of a group suicide? Also, why did none of the disciples question this situation? Was Sot'aesan charismatic enough to put all doubts to rest? Did all the disciples really have no qualms about dying?

Moreover, how is one to know whether permission was received from the netherworld? What exactly is the 'other world?' Is it really like what one prophet said, that it is a world in which deities who control this world discuss together how to make the world of humans a better place? Most importantly, was there really a blood stamp? How could this have happened if the fingerprints were made by bare hands without ink? This is impossible under the laws of nature, but it is not always correct to assume that nothing occurs outside the boundaries of natural law. With these questions in mind, we must move on to the next topic. It is said that Sot'aesan later burned the paper with the blood stamp on it. Sot'aesan, who strongly disliked performing supernatural feats, did not want people to be restricted by the 'power' of the paper.

In Preparation for True Work

Sot'aesan had now completed all the necessary preparations. He had fully trained his disciples' body and soul. All that was left to do was to go out into the world. His first act was not to go around declaring that the world was coming to an end the way Jesus did, but go about his work quietly in the typical manner of an Eastern sage. The first things that the conscientious and fully prepared Sot'aesan did were the canonization of doctrine and the establishment of his religion's infrastructure. To achieve this, Sot'aesan went into one of the various small Buddhist temples on Mount Byŏn, a mountain near his home, and spent his days there in quiet mental training. Here, Sot'aesan and his disciples laid out the basic doctrinal framework of Won Buddhism; this became the foundation for the Buddhist Dharma Society created in 1924, which establishes the pillars of Won Buddhism and publishes Won Buddhist scripture.

A Dragon in Hiding

The period of mental training at Mount Byŏn produced no visible output. It is still nevertheless a very important period in early Won Buddhist history because it is during this time that the most basic Won Buddhist doctrines were drafted. This will be explained again in a later section, but the most fundamental doctrines, like the Four Graces and directions on how to meditate, all appear during this period. Of course, it was several years later when headquarters were built in Iksan that these doctrines were formally published in scriptural format. Also, a critical evaluation of the weaknesses of traditional Buddhism entitled *A Treatise on the Reformation of Korean Buddhism* was drafted at this time. From this perspective, Sot'aesan's duration on Mount Byŏn can be seen as preparation for take-off. It was a period of waiting—the way a dragon hides in the water waiting for the time to rise to heaven—and a period for setting the foundations in place and accumulating substance.[3] After four to five years of this type of waiting, the 'dragon' leaps out of the water. But first let us take a look at the period on Mount Byŏn.

3 Dragons in Eastern cultures are very different from the evil monsters depicted in European fairy tales. In ancient China and Korea it was the symbol of the emperor. A dragon is believed to lie dormant in the sea until it is time for it to rise to heaven.

Stories from Mount Byŏn

There are several interesting anecdotes about Sot'aesan's time on Mount Byŏn that I would like to introduce here. There was a monk, Zen Master Hakmyŏng, who Sot'aesan considered a training colleague. When he heard that Hakmyŏng was coming to the mountain, Sot'aesan instructed a thirteen-year-old boy in the art of Zen riddle, or *koan*. The monk soon arrived and exchanged a few *koan* with the boy. Of course, the boy answered exactly the way he had been taught by Sot'aesan. For example, in response to the question "What is the true meaning of dharma," he would raise one finger. Hakmyŏng declared that the boy was enlightened and formally acknowledged him. At this, Sot'aesan appeared from where he had been hiding and pointed out that this was no longer a good method. What does this mean? Sot'aesan was implying that certain *koan* answers had become common. Thus, even children could become acknowledged if they simply answered as they were told. The purpose of *koan* question and answer is to shatter deeply ingrained preconception of daily life, but ironically this itself had become standardized. Examples of this are easy to find today in our own surroundings. You can see that most of those who supposedly do mental training have fallen victim to this very mannerism. Because there is no inner voice to be heard, they grow out their hair and beards and go around in strange clothing as if to compensate for what they lack. I believe that Sot'aesan wanted to counter this kind of false approach.

On a different note, I feel it necessary to introduce Sot'aesan's own evaluation of his time in hiding. Upon hearing that an enlightened sage was residing at Mount Byŏn, several conscientious youth came to visit Sot'aesan. The point of their argument was simple. If Sot'aesan was truly enlightened, then he should be out helping the independence movement instead of hiding in a remote rural village. Sot'aesan's reply is instructive. If a person wanting to catch fish in the Pacific tries to do this by beating the fish with a stick, how much would he end up catching? What Sot'aesan meant was that instead of beating the fish, it would be much more productive to make as large of a net as possible, even if this would take some time. Then what does this net refer to? It was probably the organization of Won Buddhism itself and canonization of doctrine. As we saw in Chapter 1, Sot'aesan endured a great deal of suffering to become enlightened and thus became aware of many things. But none of this had been organized into doctrine. For this to be possible, one must take time to reflect upon what has been stored deep inside the mind and shape it so that it can be shared with others. Sot'aesan probably also needed time to mentally recharge. He probably thought over and over again about how he wanted to go about his work in the future.

As mentioned previously, Sot'aesan once said that of the many religious works in his previous lives, this one was by far the largest in scale. How are we to understand this? Because of his firmly Buddhist roots, Sot'aesan firmly believed in reincarnation, the wheel of life that is determined by *karma*. Within this frame of reference, how should we interpret Sot'aesan's declaration that it had taken several lives to come up with his current work? Do enlightened teachers continuously reappear? Did Jesus and Buddha return to this world after they left? A mere sentient being like myself cannot help but have such questions. In any case, because this was Sot'aesan's biggest work yet, he must have needed time to sort out his thoughts. Sot'aesan ends up spending a lengthy four years at Mount Byŏn. During this time, basic Won Buddhist doctrine such as the replacement of the Buddha statue with the

Il-Won-Sang (one circle image) would be formulated.

The Story of the Buddhist Mass

When discussing Sot'aesan's duration at Mount Byŏn, one cannot leave out the true story of the Buddhist mass. Sot'aesan never wasted an opportunity to criticize the worship of lifeless Buddha statues; the story of the Buddhist mass stands out because it is directly related to this concept. The story itself is straight-forward. Sot'aesan saw an elderly couple on the road and for some reason stopped to ask them where they were going. The couple replied that they were going to the temple to give mass because their daughter-in-law was too disobedient. Sot'aesan offered the following radical reply. "You offer mass to a lifeless Buddha statue, but why do you not offer mass to a living Buddha?" At the elderly couple's surprise, Sot'aesan answered, "Your daughter-in-law is the living Buddha. This is the Buddha to whom you should offer mass. There is no need to do this for a mere statue. It is your daughter-in-law who has the ability to exercise filial piety." When the couple asked what they should do, Sot'aesan advised that they spend the money they were going to use for the Buddhist mass to buy a nice present for their daughter-in-law.

The ending of the story is unremarkable. When the elderly couple bought a present for their daughter-in-law every week, the daughter-in-law remained suspicious at first but was later won over, repented completely and became a new person. Of course, the story ended happily as the couple and their daughter-in-law become devoted to one another. This type of story is also common in the Buddhist tradition, but it better matches the philosophy of Won Buddhism, which rejects worship of Buddha images. Moreover, this story is much more vivid because it mentions actual places and names. While the story is moving, there is nothing more difficult than to actually practice this in daily life. We ordinary people are so quick to turn our backs when someone has committed even a slight wrong; it is a truly difficult task to go out of our way to do something for that person. Sot'aesan told another story. In discussing the difference between a mere fellow and a bodhisattva, he stated that a mere fellow dislikes someone for having committed one wrong after ten good deeds, but a bodhisattva is grateful for one good deed out of ten wrongdoings. This proves that the vast majority of us are merely fellows. Is enlightenment such a long road as this?

The Dragon Rises Up

The Creation of the Buddhist Dharma Society

After having spent four years as a dragon in hiding, Sot'aesan expresses his desire to go out into the world in 1924. His first act was to create the Buddhist Dharma Society. The name of course indicates the belief that Buddhism is the foundational underpinning of Won Buddhism, but it also reflects the reality of the day. At the height of the colonial period, it was difficult to obtain recognition from the Japanese colonial government for any religion except Buddhism. Until the name is changed to Won Buddhism after liberation by second Prime Dharma Master Chŏngsan, the responsibility of leading the Buddhist Dharma Society weighed heavy on Sot'aesan's shoulders.

In deciding the site of the group, there is one thing that is difficult to understand. Various sites must have been considered, but the final decision was the city of Iksan, the current location of Won Buddhist central headquarters. Why was an open field on the outskirts of Iksan chosen over the more developed Chŏnju? The site of the current headquarters is still a quiet place with little traffic; it makes me wonder what it must have been like ninety years ago. But Sot'aesan, in character, had a different opinion. He argued that although the site was currently (in 1924) bare and remote, the entire world would turn its eyes toward this place. He prophesized that the amount of traffic would increase and many people from other countries would visit, making Iksan the center of Buddhadharma. Sot'aesan's prophesy has not been realized to the exact letter, but a significant portion of it has been achieved. Now that Iksan has become synonymous to 'home of Won Buddhism' and many international conferences have been held there, we can see that Sot'aesan's prophesy was not a false one.

The number of believers at this time is also worthy of note. It had already been nine years since Sot'aesan became enlightened. There were 130 members (male and female combined) and 13 ministers. The term 'minister' (*kyomu*) refers to those who have entered the Won Buddhist order. Ministers work exclusively on the internal affairs of the order. We can conclude that although there were not many lay believers, the number of ordained ministers was relatively high. There is nothing unusual about a religion having few believers in its early stage. During the first few decades when Mohammed, the founder of Islam, was still in charge, there were less than ten believers. In comparison, the fact that there were 13 ministers is remarkable because these people can in turn teach hundreds or thousands of others. Since then, Won Buddhism has grown to the extent that it is today one of the four major religions of Korea. This clearly shows that having only a few believers at the beginning stages is not an obstacle to future growth.

Sot'aesan's Next Disciple: Presbyterian Elder Cho

There are many stories about those who became ministers at this time, but the most dramatic of these by far is the story of Songkwang Cho, a Presbyterian elder who became Sot'aesan's disciple and rose to become a minister. Cho was originally a follower of Tonghak but later converted to Christianity. He became an avid believer with a strong social conscience and established churches as well as schools for underprivileged teens. He was determined to learn medicine so that he could heal the sick just as Jesus had done. In other words, Cho was an enthusiastic Christian. I believe that this enthusiasm stemmed from being caught up by fundamental religious questions. It is said that while he was busily involved in social activities, he continuously asked himself, "What is my current stance? Where am I going now?" Cho was approached by Chŏkbyŏk Song, an individual who appears frequently in early Won Buddhist history who recommended him several times to visit Sot'aesan. At times like this, a person seems to be reduced to two options: 'there is nothing to lose' or 'even if this is a hoax, I will at least learn something.'

The person who remembers this meeting most accurately is Elder Cho's daughter, another vital individual in Won Buddhist history who eventually becomes the first female minister. Upon hearing that her father had fallen into the clutches of the leader of a strange new religion—a youth fifteen years his junior, at that—she goes to Sot'aesan to save her father. No doubt a devout Christian herself, in her mind it was clear that her father, a respectable elder of the church, had fallen victim to Satan. But even this daughter, who had set off enraged and determined to gain her father back, is eventually also won over by Sot'aesan and becomes his disciple. Her three daughters and her son-in-law all become ministers, forming a truly devout Won Buddhist family. Her memory of the meeting between her father and Sot'aesan is as follows.

It seems that Elder Cho made a bet with Sot'aesan that after asking each other questions, the person who was unable to answer would become the disciple of the other. The questions and answers were the following. When Sot'aesan asks Cho whether he had ever seen and heard God and received his teaching, Cho answers in the negative. Sot'aesan replies that Cho has not yet become a core disciple of Jesus, and that if he studies hard enough it will be possible. As words continued to be exchanged back and forth, Cho was apparently genuinely taken by Sot'aesan. Upon asking to become Sot'aesan's disciple, Cho expresses unease about becoming a traitor to his religion. Sot'aesan reassured Cho that becoming his disciple was the same as becoming a disciple of Jesus. At this, Cho bowed three times, demonstrating his acceptance of Sot'aesan as his teacher. But Sot'aesan did not immediately accept Cho into the fold. He wanted to give Cho some more time to think. Several months later, Cho does officially enter the Buddhist Dharma Society. Moreover, family members who had objected to Cho's conversion began to one at a time follow his path.

This story is suggestive of many things. The conversation between the two men reveals Sot'aesan's absolute realism (his thoughts about the existence of God), but that discussion is a highly technical one that we will not explore further in this book. We will instead focus on the extraordinary meeting itself. Firstly, the fact that a sophisticated believer like Elder Cho voluntarily became Sot'aesan's disciple reveals the depth of enlightenment of the latter. People like us who are not enlightened are hard-pressed to recognize this in others, but those who are enlightened can easily identify one another. As with other issues related to enlightenment, the only way we can attempt to draw any type of conclusion is through circumstantial facts. The meeting that we have just observed is solid evidence that shows the depth and breadth of Sot'aesan's capacity.

These two prominent religious figures conversed for two hours without one being defeated by the other, and Sot'aesan was able to win over a Presbyterian elder fifteen years his senior. This shows that Sot'aesan was extraordinary in every sense of the word. Within a Confucian society rigidly ruled by laws on age seniority, it must have been no easy feat to overcome a fifteen year age difference. In short, Sot'aesan's words were convincing enough for Songkwang Cho, a doctor of Oriental medicine and a church elder, to bow three times to him on the spot. In addition, Sot'aesan does not immediately accept Cho even after he has become convinced; he instead gives Cho plenty of time to think over his decision, showing that Sot'aesan was truly enlightened. One common tendency of leaders of pseudo religions is that they insist "all things will be solved if you come to me." There is no solicitous discretion or respect of the other's position like that displayed by Sot'aesan. The same was true of Buddha as well. A disciple of Mahavira, the founder of Jainism, was moved by Buddha and asked the latter to become his disciple. However, in the way that only a true teacher could, Buddha sent him back to Mahavira. We will continue to see in Sot'aesan the qualities of a true teacher.

The Making of Scripture

From now until his death, Sot'aesan mainly works toward strengthening the organization of the order. Sot'aesan seems to have been a highly scrupulous and considerate and also a strict leader. I believe that Sot'aesan worried a great deal about what would happen after he was gone. In other words, with the exception of a few, most of the disciples were not up to his standards. Perhaps it was because of this that Sot'aesan fortified the order in various ways. There are probably few religious leaders in the history of mankind who took care of their 'flock' to the extent that Sot'aesan did for his.

There is no need to delve into too much detail the rather complicated and tedious process of how Sot'aesan reorganized his group. Of all the work that was done during this period, the project that most stands out is the preparation to publish the scriptures. In addition to these large projects, Sot'aesan also devoted his time to numerous other aspects, like deciding regulations for group training sessions. In Buddhism, monks train in one place for a set duration of time each summer and winter; accordingly, the Buddhist Dharma Society determined the timeframe for fixed-term training during this period. In addition, rules for daily training were decided as well. These very specific set of guidelines is geared toward self-assessment by the practitioner of whether one's mind is 'caught up' by thoughts or in a state of unmindfulness. We will take a closer look at these rules in a later section.

Sot'aesan also carried out a large-scale renovation of ritual protocol. Religious rituals may not seem important to outsiders, but for lay believers of that religion these are an extremely important part of religious life. Sot'aesan probably decided to do something about it because rituals often become either too complicated, as in the case of Confucian ancestral rites, or, as in the case of Buddhism, fail to address even basic needs like weddings. As a result, Won Buddhist ritual undergoes a transformation that renders them very simple and full of symbolic elements. This can be seen in the practice of substituting food with clean water, which is passed down to his central disciple Chŏngsan. Chŏngsan brings up a practical argument against the Confucian practice of setting out food during ancestral rites. He is the one who pointed out that if people truly believed that the ancestral spirits eat the food, it should be set out every day instead of only on the day the rites are performed. Chŏngsan directed that fresh water be used instead. This tradition, already practiced in Tonghak, seems to have been borrowed from it. Not only is the content of the food often subject to dispute, but there are often differences between social class and economic means; perhaps Chŏngsan's intention was to do away with all of these by insisting on using water.

No discussion of religious rituals is complete without mentioning funerals and weddings. Traditional Buddhism was indifferent on this aspect. According to Sot'aesan's critique, while traditional Buddhism created a host of rituals, it failed to do anything about funerals and weddings, the two ceremonies that people need the most. I believe this to be an accurate assessment. Of course, we cannot disregard the special circumstances of Buddhism. During the Chosŏn dynasty, the vast majority of people held weddings and funerals in the Confucian tradition, eliminating any need to go to a temple. As a result, monks probably saw no need to create any guidelines. However, even today, Buddhism does not seem to have a standardized procedure by which to conduct weddings and funerals. The reason why Sot'aesan probably spent so much time on ritual reform is his motto: "dharma as everyday life."

More than anything else, what made Sot'aesan unique as a religious founder was his passion regarding the publication of scripture. People who found religions are generally not very interested in writing or publishing scriptures: Jesus and Buddha are representative examples. There are many possible explanations, but the most convincing of these is that enlightened individuals have little interest in gathering people around them and exercising authority. In a sense, secular work is a type of greed. Because those who are enlightened are already complete, they have no desire to leave traces of themselves for the edification of future generations. They do not secretly wish that their disciples will remain to teach future generations their laws and thus continue to be worshipped long after they have left this world. The act of expecting something from someone else is endemic only to ordinary sentient beings. But Sot'aesan, contrary to popular opinion, was highly interested in his group of disciples and the publication of his scriptures. This sometimes leads to criticism that Sot'aesan was not truly enlightened.

But could these works of Sot'aesan be evaluated in a positive light? Firstly, he seems to have been a very fastidious and caring teacher. From his enlightened perspective, he had plenty of reason to be gravely concerned about his disciples. Evidence shows that his disciples caused Sot'aesan a great deal of worry and pain. On top of everything else, this was the harshest period of Japanese rule. Sot'aesan worried that without him, there was no telling when the evil Japanese would exterminate the Won Buddhist order. The Buddhist Dharma Society was constantly under a microscope for the duration of the colonial period. Amidst such circumstances, it was Sot'aesan's last wish that he at least oversee the building of the foundations so that the order would not succumb to external threat. Moreover, highly developed printing technology of the day meant that it was easy to publish a book. In Jesus or Buddha's era, this would have been impossible because of the almost non-existent status of printing technology. In the case of Sot'aesan, the abundance of advanced technology made it all too easy to publish.

The thoughts that had been formulated on Mount Byŏn first came out in book form in 1927. This is followed by the appearance of several revised editions, but ordinary readers need not know all the details. What I would like to discuss here is *Chŏngjŏn* (*The Principle Book of Won-Buddhism*), the scripture that Sot'aesan personally oversaw every step of the way. The current Won Buddhist scripture is composed of two parts: the first part is entitled *Chŏngjŏn* and the second part is entitled *Taejonggyŏng* (*The Scripture of the Founding Master*). In terms of page length, parts 1 and 2 form a 1:4 ratio. *Taejonggyŏng* was put together posthumously by Sot'aesan's disciples, and is similar in format to the four Gospels in the Christian Bible. On the other hand, *Chŏngjŏn* is a selection of core Won Buddhist doctrine. Upon reading *Chŏngjŏn*, I cannot help but wonder how the religion's most central tenets could have been outlined so succinctly yet so meticulously at the same time. The section on practice describes every aspect to an amazingly elaborate degree, even when and where to train. One can only wonder whether Buddhism had a manual for lay believers that was comprehensive and easy to understand. Firstly, directions on how to confess,—in religion, confession and repentance are very important!—pray and record a diary of one's daily training are well-organized. In addition, there are explanations on how to make Buddha offerings, directions on how to train by alternately doing seated meditation and reciting Buddha's name, and even which *koan* to use while meditating. This will all be revisited later in the chapter on doctrine. In my lifetime I have not seen a more helpful and detailed religious training manual.

Sot'aesan probably felt compelled to explain himself to such lengths because his disciples did not put his mind at ease. He did not want his hard-earned teachings to be lost due to the inadequacy of his disciples. Let us see what Sot'aesan was thinking at the time: "My head hurts so much because of you people; it feels like it's burning up. I will be going on a trip soon, so you must hurry and work hard. You folks can't write *Chŏngjŏn* by yourselves. So make it while I'm still around."[4] Related by a disciple who was present when Sot'aesan spoke these words, it offers various interesting insights. Firstly, this short statement reveals Sot'aesan's 'human' side. We often think that enlightened people will always act in a holy and stately manner, but this is usually not the case. For example, Buddhists today believe that Buddha was a holy person, but he was also apparently very fastidious. One anecdote notes that right after Buddha's death, one of his closest disciples gleefully said "the old man who never stopped nagging us is finally dead." Sot'aesan's above statement is along the same lines; it is made colorful and vivid because Sot'aesan does not use the dignified tone of the scriptures but instead is busy chastising his disciples, who never seem to catch up to his standards. When addressing his disciples, Sot'aesan does not use a formal term like 'gentlemen' but a much more intimate term in Korean that is closest in English to 'you folks.' His comment that "my head hurts so much because of you people" is also highly amusing. From his enlightened perspective, the disciples must all have seemed like thoughtless children. One can indirectly feel the frustration behind his homespun words. "Going on a trip" indicates that Sot'aesan will soon be leaving this world,

4 Yongduk Park, *Chŏnha Nongpan* in *Wŏnpulkyo Ch'ogi Kyodansa* (Early Won Buddhist History) (Seoul: Dongnampoong, 1999), 329.

but his disciples did not seem to have caught on. This will be discussed again later, but Sot'aesan believed that in the face of increasing pressure from the Japanese, his prompt death was essential for the survival of the order. He died at the age of 53, a relatively young age for the founder of a religion. Thus, Sot'aesan was in a hurry. He tried urging on his disciples, but was frustrated by their lack of ability.

Amidst such tumultuous times, *Chŏngjŏn* was at last completed. However, as the Korean proverb goes, "beyond this mountain, there is another mountain." The Japanese colonial government, naming one irrelevant objection after another, refused to allow the publication of this scripture. They used whatever objections they possibly could to put up obstacles, like the fact that there were no verses praising the emperor and that it was not written in Japanese. Sot'aesan wrote that he strongly opposed writing a Japanese version of *Chŏngjŏn.* According to him, this was because the Japanese language would soon disappear. He probably foresaw the downfall of the Japanese empire. As his disciples grew increasingly nervous with the repeated delaying of publication, Sot'aesan reassured them that "even if we are forced to close our doors, we can hide in the mountains for a while because we have the draft of *Chŏngjŏn*;" this shows how attached Sot'aesan was to these scriptures. The heavens eventually came to his aid. Taehŭp Kim, president of a Buddhist publishing house, offered to publish the scripture under his own name. Kim, who had always admired Sot'aesan, heard of the Won Buddhist order's publication difficulties and offered his own name as an expedient. But *Chŏngjŏn* was not to be published in Sot'aesan's lifetime. Upon hearing that it had received a publication permit, Sot'aesan prepared for his nirvana. Precisely speaking, Sot'aesan dies one month before the

Principle Book comes out in published form. The Won Buddhist scripture that we know today was published in 1962 as a combination of *Chŏngjŏn* with *Taejonggyŏng*, a collection of Sot'aesan's teachings.

Sot'aesan's Last Days

In the years just before his death, Sot'aesan often spoke of traveling to the Kŭmgang (Diamond) Mountains. His disciples had no idea that this was a foreshadowing of their teacher's nirvana. Given the intense persecution by the Japanese, Sot'aesan believed that his timely death would save the order from complete destruction. He is said to have once pointed to the Japanese police and remarked that "they are shortening my life." The oppression of that period seems to have been greater than we think. This is because the Japanese authorities were very sensitive about anything related to the Korean spirit in any shape or form. Because there was no way of knowing when and how an organization formed by Koreans would transform into an independence movement, the Japanese colonial government heavily sanctioned all groups run by Koreans.

Moreover, Sot'aesan was known to the Japanese as the 'Gandhi of Chosŏn.' He seems to have received such attention because as a religious leader, he could not exercise armed resistance and instead resorted to nonviolence and nonresistance. Because of his growing fame, there were supposedly many voices within the Japanese police force that wanted to eliminate the Buddhist Dharma Society before it grew too big to control. This led Sot'aesan to think that his death would allow the order to survive. When he died in 1943, Japanese authorities are said to have remarked, "It is now over. Now that the founder is dead, the Buddhist Dharma Society will self-destruct."

Sot'aesan was no doubt in poor health. He had a severe cough because of his excessively intense training. Not only did he suffer from coughing sickness for the rest of his life, but Sot'aesan also had other ailments like frequent colds and frequently turning red. However, his early death was most likely not only caused by his poor physical health. Is it not true that enlightened people are able to control the length of their lives? It is a time-honored belief that they choose when to enter the world as well the exact hour of their departure. Sot'aesan probably fits into this category.

While he prepared to die, Sot'aesan delivered his last Transmission Verse in 1941, two years before his death. Famous within the Won Buddhist order, it is included in the *Il-Won-Sang* vow that all believers read aloud each morning and evening. The content is very short: "Being into nonbeing and nonbeing into being, Turning and turning—in the ultimate, Being and nonbeing are both void, Yet this void is also complete." It is a short but profound statement. The turning of being and nonbeing refers to the mysterious cycle in which all things in the universe are born and then die. The fact that change occurs in things that are in fact 'void' reflects heavy Buddhist influence. "Being and nonbeing are both void" does not actually mean that there is nothing, but can be understood as a 'filled emptiness' or that no substance is fixed. Sot'aesan emphasized that in the past, teachers would only pass on such teachings secretly to their core disciples, but he himself opened this up to all who wanted to learn—a more democratic transmission. The establishment of the *Il-Won-Sang* inside the temple in 1935 for the first time in Won Buddhist history received a great deal of attention for a time. All rituals thereafter would have been carried out centered on the *Il-Won-Sang*; we will take a much closer look at this in the following chapter.

There is nothing in Sot'aesan's death that looks special. Having been ill all the while, Sot'aesan checked into a hospital in May 1943 and quietly died in early June. It is said that Sot'aesan had been seated and was talking to a visitor when he took his last breath and slumped onto the floor. For an enlightened man, it was a rather nondescript nirvana. Someone able to freely navigate life and death could have called together all his disciples and told them "Now that I will soon be leaving, ask me one last question." After giving his last dharma talk, he would then have passed quietly into nirvana in a sitting position.[5] But Sot'aesan did not follow this method at all, the reason for which we ordinary people could never understand. As stated previously, the Iksan police department jumped for joy at Sot'aesan's death. They were confident that the Buddhist Dharma Society would soon disappear, no longer requiring their constant surveillance. But Sot'aesan had already trained his successor Chŏngsan as the next Prime Dharma Master. Thus, ecclesiastical authority was able to be handed down without incident and the order has continued to develop ever since.

One story that must be told about Sot'aesan's death is about the sermon given by Ueno, the head priest of Pakmun Temple (Hirobumi-ji Temple in Japanese), on the forty-ninth day after the death. Won-Buddhism (the Buddhist Dharma Society) had close relations with Pakmun Temple for a variety of reasons. We will discuss this relationship later and for now focus on what Ueno said in his sermon. Ueno seems to have been greatly moved by

5 In the Zen Buddhist tradition, the ideal way to die is while meditating, which would mean that one would have to be seated rather than lying in bed.

Sot'aesan's personality after several meetings with him. Unable to contain his sobs, Ueno declared in his sermon at the forty-ninth day ritual that "Sot'aesan is greater than Dōgen, the founder of Sotoshū." Most books on Won Buddhist history do not further elaborate on this comment, but if this statement was actually made, it is truly remarkable compliment. To comprehend the weight of this compliment, one first needs an understanding of Japanese Buddhism.

Pakmun Temple was affiliated with Sotoshū, a Buddhist denomination that had a considerable power base in Japan at the time. The Japanese colonial government chose to build a temple in honor of Ito Hirobumi within this group.[6] This shows that Sotoshū's rich history within the Japanese Buddhist tradition. This very Sotoshū was founded by Dōgen, who is acknowledged today by Buddhist academia all over the world as a world-class philosopher for the depth and originality of his teachings. Even when I was in graduate school in the US in the 1980s, I took a seminar on Dōgen which used an English translation of his teachings. I remember how enthusiastically my advisor, Professor Charles Fu, lectured on a comparison of Dōgen's writings and Heidegger's *Being and Time*. Although I no longer remember all the details, I received the general impression that Dōgen was a highly original and innovative thinker. My advisor argued that Dōgen had more advanced views on time and existence than Heidegger, which sounded fairly convincing at the time. Simply speaking, Dōgen was one of the world's top philosophers and the darling of Buddhist

6 Ito Hirobumi was an elder statesman who was sent to Chosŏn to conclude the Protectorate Treaty of 1905, which gave Japan full authority over Korea's foreign relations. Slated to be the first Governor General of Korea, Hirobumi never realized this goal. He was shot by patriot Chung-gŭn An in 1909.

studies everywhere.

It was in comparison to this Dōgen that Sot'aesan was ranked more highly. It is rather childish to try to determine who is 'better' than whom, but head priest Ueno of Pakmun Temple was obviously influenced to that extent by the towering personality of Sot'aesan. Ueno was an influential monk of a popular denomination in a colonial power. The fact that he praised an unknown philosopher of his country's colony so highly indicates a victory of Sot'aesan's greatness. Some say that although Sot'aesan's philosophy is comprehensive, it does not seem very original because so much of its content is mundane and ordinary. In other words, it seems too simple. This reaction is typical of scholars who only study esoteric scriptures and completely misunderstand the nature of religion itself. Religious leaders of the highest rank do not use difficult language. Take for example the teachings of Jesus. How is it difficult-sounding in any way? Look at how these simple teachings have developed into Thomas Aquinas' notoriously difficult theology and Alfred North Whitehead's Process Theology (if this can be called development)! The same is true for Buddha. Who would have known that the sermons of the earliest Buddhist scriptures, which are so easy to understand, would develop into the School of the Middle Way and the School of Mere Consciousness, the most complicated philosophies in the world? I believe that Sot'aesan's teachings are in the same category. Only time will tell how far it will be developed and how it will be reinterpreted.

Won Buddhism in the Colonial Period

We have thus far done a fairly detailed study of Sot'aesan and his life. It is now time to move onto his disciple Chŏngsan, but let us first take a short break with stories of several incidents from the colonial period.

Won Buddhist historical records show that the efforts of the Japanese to break up the Won Buddhist order were tenacious beyond belief. One can only exclaim at the wisdom and preparedness of Sot'aesan in dealing with such pressure. The Japanese authorities oppressed the order in various ways that cannot all be discussed here. One time, a member of the police conducted an internal investigation on the grounds that because men and women lived in the same space, there must be something unsavory going on. Having considered the ramifications of this long before, it is said that Sot'aesan required an old man to be present when members of the opposite sex met, no matter how close the relationship may be. This eliminated any cause for suspicion. There is also an incident on financial matters in which the Japanese authorities, confident that there must be some degree of embezzlement, minutely examined all of the order's ledgers. Won Buddhist records state that the investigation revealed no miscalculation of even a single cent. The Japanese probably looked into these matters because most 'similar' religious groups were caught for problems involving women and lack of financial transparency.

There were also ideological issues. The biggest concern of the Japanese at the time was whether an organization was connected to socialism or communism. As the Won Buddhist order radically reformed traditional rituals, lived communally, and took an interest in social welfare facilities like nursing homes and orphanages, it was suspected to be linked to socialism. Of course, the order's innocence was reconfirmed. With no problem discovered on this regard, the next area of attack was Won Buddhist doctrine itself.

There is one extreme incident related to this that I feel compelled to share. One day in 1938, colonial government officials, the North Chŏlla police force and senior officials of the Iksan police station barged into headquarters in two cars. Upon meeting Sot'aesan, they grilled him with the following question. Why did he have ancestral tablets for the Fourfold Graces of heaven and earth, parents, fellow beings and laws, but nothing to commemorate the magnanimity of the (Japanese) emperor? In those circumstances, it may have been an obvious question. But Sot'aesan was not to be easily moved. All Buddhists receive the grace of Buddha, but this is not expressed in writing. In the same way, as citizens of the Japanese empire, is it not given that the grace of the emperor is appreciated? His logic was that there was no reason for something as obvious as the grace of Buddha or the emperor to be worshipped separately. In this way, immediate danger was successfully averted.

We cannot avoid mention of the Name Order, an edict which required all Koreans to change to Japanese surnames. Won Buddhists were no exception, but Sot'aesan managed to overcome this crisis as well. Sot'aesan's rule of thumb in responding to such crises was to never go against the command. Changing one's last name had already become a social trend: avoiding it could shake the very foundations of the order. After the Name Order was issued in 1941, almost 90 percent of Koreans had changed their last names within a year and a half. Thus, Sot'aesan could not hope to stand alone on this matter, but nor could he simply acquiesce to the demands of the Japanese. Sot'aesan devises an incredible exit strategy. While deciding that everyone would indeed change their names, it would be done strictly according to Won Buddhist ways. Sot'aesan's Japanese name is Ilwon Chŭngsa, which means 'an enlightened being who knows the truth of Ilwon.' This name actually seems more befitting than his real name. In this way, Sot'aesan found a middle ground on which he could preserve his principles while avoiding confrontation with the Japanese authorities. Thereafter, many of Sot'aesan's disciples including Chŏngsan followed suit by changing their last names to Ilwon as well.

There were countless more such moments, but of these the incident on the audience with the Japanese Heavenly Emperor is particularly noteworthy. The Japanese colonial government, wanting to incite apostasy among Korean leaders of various popular movements, arranged for them to meet the Japanese emperor. The message was that because the Japanese Heavenly Emperor is even higher than an emperor, an audience with him should be enough to eliminate undesirable elements like the independence movement. This strategy apparently had some effect because there were several who were genuinely moved by the 'grace' of the Japanese ruler. This tremendous honor (?) was given to Sot'aesan as well. When presented with this request, Sot'aesan immediately replied affirmatively without any hesitation. When faced with a situation that they know they cannot do anything about, mature personalities like Sot'aesan try to find a solution for it rather than oppose it point- blank; this is probably why Sot'aesan was able to respond on the spot. Moreover, any sign of hesitation for an invitation of this magnitude could be interpreted as sedition and make the Japanese authorities even more suspicious. However, this was where Sot'aesan's cooperation ended. From that point on, Sot'aesan employed countless dilatory measures to avoid the demands of the Japanese. After going to Pusan as if he would leave immediately for Japan (Pusan is a port city in Korea's southernmost province from which people would travel to Japan by boat), he delayed his 'departure' date several times with various excuses.

However, he could not delay the trip forever. Sot'aesan next comes down with an eye infection. Although we cannot know whether the eye infection was intentional or not, he uses it as a legitimate excuse to refuse an audience with the Japanese emperor. The reasoning was along the lines of "how can I possibly request to see His Majesty the Emperor with such blasphemous eyes." This true story fortunately worked out. As more time went by with this reason, this time the Japanese colonial government informed Sot'aesan that he need not go to Japan. Sot'aesan's plan was a success.

The Won Buddhist order resorted to various measures to survive the constant pressure from the Japanese, some of which were truly heartrending. Among these, the hanging up of a Buddhist temple nameplate was a tragic day.[7] The incident occurred as follows. With the transition to a wartime government toward the end of the colonial period, the order was commanded by the Japanese to actively cooperate in the war effort. But the order did not do this, and soon faced the very real possibility of dissolution. Then, some voices from within the order suggested that as a last resort, the group could camouflage itself as a branch of the main Japanese temple in Seoul. Upon inquiring, they were put in contact with the head priest of Pakmun Temple in Seoul, who was briefly mentioned earlier in this chapter. The Won Buddhists eventually succeeded in receiving a nameplate from the temple. Pakmun Temple, located where the Shilla Hotel stands today, was built in honor of the Japanese hero Ito Hirobumi. The Japanese colonial government placed great significance on this temple, even laying streetcar tracks directly in front of the temple. Becoming the

---

7 In Mahayana Buddhism (Korea and Japan in particular), the name of the temple is written in Chinese characters on a large wooden plate. This is hung at the center of the main entrance gate.

branch of this temple would prevent even the Japanese from threatening them, according to Won Buddhist logic. While the attempt was a success, it does not seem to have had much effect. Thereafter, the Japanese authorities, instead of trying to eliminate the Won Buddhist order, decided to convert it to the so-called 'Heavenly Emperor Buddhism.' During this stage, Sot'aesan dies and the next leader Chŏngsan resists the Japanese to the very end. When all the preparations to convert to Heavenly Emperor Buddhism were complete and all that remained was for Prime Dharma Master Chŏngsan to stamp his seal on the documents, he puts forth an excuse and goes off traveling in the countryside. It was a delaying tactic, just as Sot'aesan had done. To make matters worse, a regiment of the Japanese army stationed itself in Iksan headquarters. The fate of Won Buddhism looked as good as dead. All of this came to an end with liberation on August 15, 1945.

Depending on the person, there are slight differences in opinion regarding whether or not the order at the time was a Japanese sympathizer. However, there were no incidents in which Won Buddhist leaders encouraged young people to fight on the battlefield or sign up for labor mobilization. If this is indeed true, it is a remarkable feat. Almost all political and intellectual leaders of Korea at that time were Japanese mouthpieces in terms of wartime mobilization, but there are no records that give any indication that Sot'aesan or his disciples were involved with this. This shows the group's strong mental solidarity.

One last story I would like to share about the colonial period is that of Kabong Hwang, a Korean police officer in the Japanese police force who investigated the order for five years. Hwang was later given the Buddhist name Ichŏn and became Sot'aesan's disciple. We have already seen the extent of Japanese persecution of Won Buddhism. Within central headquarters, there was a small cave-like opening dug below the room where sermons were given; when Sot'aesan gave a sermon, Japanese detectives would listen to everything he said from there. But later anecdotes state that Sot'aesan treated even these detectives with generosity of heart. Sot'aesan often said, "Just as I do my work, the detectives are doing theirs." Of those detectives, Ichŏn (Kabong) Hwang was eventually won over by Sot'aesan's teachings and became a disciple. Of the many detectives who sat watch, Ichŏn was the only one who was linked to Won Buddhism by providence. Buddha once said that no matter how talented, no one who is not destined to be saved can be saved. Ichŏn Hwang obviously had a strong predestined bond with Sot'aesan; both of his children received ordination into the priesthood. Ichŏn himself formally became a believer after liberation and contributed to Sot'aesan's oral records until his death in 1990 (born in 1910).

Second Prime Dharma Master, Chŏngsan

Before we conclude this chapter, there is one more person who needs mentioning: second Prime Dharma Master Chŏngsan, born as Kyu Song (1900–1961). While Sot'aesan founded Won Buddhism, it was Chŏngsan who formed the pillars and made it into the religion it is today. I have thus far used the term 'Won Buddhism,' but technically this should have been 'Buddhist Dharma Society.' The first term was used instead of the latter in order to minimize any confusion on the reader's part. The name 'Won Buddhism' was made by Chŏngsan in 1947 after he became Prime Dharma Master. But this is not all. Any discussion of Won

Buddhism must include Wonkwang University; it was Chŏngsan who built it in Iksan, an obscure rural village. The story behind it sounds closer to myth than reality. Considering that Iksan is still rather remote even today, it would have been impossible for an ordinary person to attempt building a university on the furthest outskirts of such a place. Of course, the school did not start out as large-scale as it is today. It began with just two rooms and a sign with the name Yuil Hakrim in Chinese characters, which grew until it became a premier rural private school. Chŏngsan probably never imagined that the school would become so big. His works continue to bear fruit today.

As the American expression, no amount of emphasis is too much regarding the centrality of scripture in religion. Won Buddhism's central scripture, *The Principle Book of Won-Buddhism*, was completed during Sot'aesan's lifetime, but it only contains the most important doctrines. There are no colorful anecdotes that embody Prime Dharma Master Sot'aesan's persona. People often experience religious transformation not by studying doctrine but through personal meetings. This is why Christian scripture is centered on Jesus' deeds. In 1956 Chŏngsan began to compile a collection of Sot'aesan's sayings and acts called *The Scripture of the Founding Master*, which occupies the center of the current Won Buddhist scripture. Thus, it is unthinkable to avoid special mention of Chŏngsan when discussing Won Buddhism. Without him, Won Buddhism as we know it today would not have existed. The relationship between Sot'aesan and Chŏngsan is like the sun and moon, having formed Won Buddhism by complementing each other's roles. By meeting Chŏngsan, we will see that Sot'aesan was the most important event of his life.

Before Meeting Sot'aesan

We do not need to study Chŏngsan as closely as we did for Sot'aesan, because much of their lives overlap. In fact, there is little to say about Chŏngsan's life after excluding his relationship with Sot'aesan; records on Chŏngsan are usually organized around the latter. However, in his life before meeting Sot'aesan, various interesting stories are told about relationships with the wife, daughters and disciples of Chŭngsan, a great religious leader who came before Sot'aesan. The stories become more valuable when considering that they reveal glimpses of folk Taoism at the time. It never ceases to amaze me that there were people less than a century ago who, despite poverty, persistently searched for truth in this dangerous and fleeting world to discover the ultimate meaning of life. Chŏngsan was at the center of these efforts.

Chŏngsan was born in 1900, the very beginning of the twentieth century. His birthplace is a city called Sŏngju in North Kyŏngsang Province. Almost nothing is known about his childhood except for the fact that although he dabbled in the Chinese classics, Chŏngsan was not interested in books. Married even before adolescence at the young age of 13, this was an important turning point for Chŏngsan because it is after meeting various in-laws that he begins religious training in earnest. It seems that Chŏngsan had a respect for training from a very early age. He would sometimes pray for long periods of time, and on other occasions become so frustrated because of his many unanswered questions about training that he would drink rice wine and, being young, would be chastised for it.

The year he turned 18, Chŏngsan heard that a member of his wife's family named Yeo was highly practiced in training. He set off for Mount Kaya in order to meet Yeo, marking the beginning of his path to truth. But Chŏngsan met not Yeo but practitioners of Chŭngsando who were conducting rituals in Chŭngsando fashion. Chŏngsan trained with them several times. The practitioners then gave him an interesting piece of advice: they say that to find a teacher, one must not search in '*hado* (lower region)' but in '*sangdo* (higher region).' '*Hado*' means Kyŏngsang Province and '*sangdo*' means Chŏlla Province. To discover truth, Chŏngsan goes back and forth between his home in Kyŏngsang Province and his training grounds in Chŏlla Province. In the midst of this he enters Taewon Temple in Chŏlla Province. Here he meets Haeun Kim, a female follower, who eventually connects him to Sot'aesan.

After meeting Chŏngsan at Taewon Temple, Kim is impressed by his character and invites him to stay at her home. It is during his stay at Kim's home that Chŏngsan later recalled seeing visions of a great teacher. This teacher, of course, is Sot'aesan. These two had known in advance that they were to meet. Sot'aesan, who was in Yŏngkwang (another city in Chŏlla Province) at the time, had chosen only eight disciples, leaving open the position of central disciple. He declared to the eight that the disciple to come would do great things for Won Buddhism. Sot'aesan instructed his disciples to search for this person and often went to the mountain to obtain energy from the heavens. Chŏngsan was apparently also aware of this energy. It is said that the two almost met at a predetermined location, but this meeting did not occur because both knew that the time was not yet right. Ten months passed. One day when Sot'aesan had climbed the mountain midway and was searching the heavenly energy, he learned that the person they were waiting for was not far away. He then walked 30 miles with his disciples to where Chŏngsan was staying. There is no way of knowing how he found this house, but nevertheless it is at Haeun Kim's home that Chŏngsan first meets Sot'aesan. How excited he must have been at the moment! The man he had seen in his dreams was now there in person. Would he not have felt all his worries and difficulties were now at an end? When looking at the process through which disciple Chŏngsan and teacher Sot'aesan met, it is of a teacher seeking out a disciple, which readers may think is strange. But this is actually the norm. By worldly logic, a disciple finds a teacher after enduring countless hardships, but those who are well-versed in the Way know that the opposite is true. The reason for this is simple. A teacher who is well-versed in the Way knows who it is that he should find and can do so, but a disciple who is still learning the Way has little chance of recognizing a teacher.

The other curiosity is whether both people really searched the energy of the heavens in order to find each other. What is it about looking at the sky and feeling its energy that provides insight into events of the future? While I am not entirely sure about heavenly energy, it is said that people who are highly versed in the Way have no difficulty sensing the currents that flow between individuals. It is an often-told story within Won Buddhism. Once when Chŏngsan was training under Sot'aesan, the former's parents came to visit their son. Just as an assistant was about to inform Chŏngsan that his parents were coming, Chŏngsan first asked of him, "Have not my parents arrived?" After this was relayed to Sot'aesan, Sot'aesan also is said to have asked, "Chŏngsan knew about (his parents), right?" Like teacher like disciple. Another time, Sot'aesan predicted that "two disciples are going to fight." At this, Chŏngsan added "of these two, one will leave the order the next day." When events played out just as they had predicted, stories passed down within the order state that even Sot'aesan was greatly impressed by Chŏngsan's acumen.

Another story relates that one day while the disciples were in the midst of Zen training, Sot'aesan covered the lightbulb with his hand and felt each disciple's head to check the energy flowing out of each one. For the disciples it must have been an eerie experience. It is said that Sot'aesan could tell the extent of their training by the color of the energy. While these are all statements from the order, it is nevertheless a valuable story regardless of its truth. It is first of all a valuable insight into the daily life of someone who is highly trained. After meeting Sot'aesan, Chŏngsan does not immediately follow him but waits two months before going to Yŏngkwang.

After meeting Sot'aesan

The true beginning of Chŏngsan's life was the moment he met Sot'aesan. Chŏngsan was born in order to meet Sot'aesan and set the Won Buddhist order on a solid foundation. He once said that there were two joyful events in his life: the first was being born in Korea and the second was having met Sot'aesan. Does it not make sense that the former is because of the latter? As Chŏngsan himself admitted, Sot'aesan was his entire life and the most important aspect of it. For a religious person, the greatest thing that can happen is to meet a true teacher and become enlightened; in that sense Chŏngsan's statement is a statement of the obvious. But here an unanswerable question comes to mind. Why is it that meetings must always occur in this world? We could meet one another as spirits while in the spirit world and take care of all our problems there. This would be so much easier compared to the difficulties of living in this world. Had Sot'aesan or Chŏngsan still been alive, this question would have been easily answered.

The first thing that Chŏngsan and Sot'aesan did after Chŏngsan arrived in Yŏngkwang was to officially cement their relationship as teacher and disciple. But instead of having Chŏngsan attend to the affairs of the order, Sot'aesan had him dig a cave in a nearby mountain and locked him into it. There were supposedly two reasons for this. The first reason was to protect Chŏngsan from being in the public eye. A tip that the central disciple was chosen from Kyŏngsang Province could attract unnecessary attention not only from the general public but the Japanese police as well. But the more important reason was to fix Chŏngsan's incorrectly done training. Chŏngsan had focused more on sorcery, including controlling the wind and rain as well as calling upon spirit generals, rather than authentic Taoism.[8] Sot'aesan believed that this kind of training could not achieve the true purpose of the Way: the ability to control life and death at will. Thus, Sot'aesan locked Chŏngsan in the cave in hopes of putting his training back on the right track. How did Sot'aesan instruct his disciple to train? Some say that Chŏngsan became sick during this time, —there are speculations that it was because of this illness that Chŏngsan died relatively young in his early 60s—meaning that the training was harsh enough that it permanently damaged Chŏngsan's health. As ordinary beings, we cannot fathom what it means to stray from the correct path in training, how such deviation affects our personalities or how this can be fixed.

---

8 In Mahayana Buddhism, the world of Buddha is believed to be guarded by spirit generals —literally, spirits who are generals.

After Sot'aesan's Passing

In 1943 Sot'aesan entered nirvana, as we have seen in a previous section. The Won Buddhist order ushered in the era of the second prime dharma master without incident. Such a peaceful power transition within a religious order is rare. The chances of there being internal disputes and power struggles in the transition from the first to the second leader are especially high; Won Buddhism can be seen as a highly exceptional case. The time gap between Sot'aesan's death and liberation was fortunately minimal, after which Won Buddhism had a successful take-off under Chŏngsan's leadership.

An event watched with keen interest at this juncture was the founding of Wonkwang University. Wongkwang University was of course originally named Yuil Hakrim. The establishment of the latter was not Chŏngsan's idea. It was Sot'aesan who planned to build the school during his lifetime and gave it the name 'Yuil.' Although Sot'aesan tried everything that he could to begin building the school, the Japanese authorities did not allow for this. Chŏngsan merely put his teacher's plans into action. How delighted Sot'aesan's spirit must have been to watch his disciple carrying out his dream to the letter! It is worthwhile to note the meaning of the school's original name. Yuil means 'sole purpose,' 'sole action' and 'sole fruit.' To analyze each meaning separately, 'sole purpose' means the salvation of this world, 'sole action' means selfless service to the public and 'sole fruit' indicates the realization of Il-won (One Circle), the ideal of Won Buddhism. In other words, the sole purpose of life is the creation of a world based on Il-won.

The establishment of a university by a religious order is a highly important work from the perspective of that organization.

The biggest advantage of establishing a religiously affiliated university is that it is a good opportunity to present the religion to the public in a positive light. This is because people generally have a good impression of a religious sect that owns a university. Secondly, there is the undeniable effect of direct or indirect evangelism. In short, there is nothing to lose and much to gain from having a university at the center of the religion. This is why most religious groups try their utmost to establish a university in their name. Two new religions that have recently succeeded in establishing universities are Daesun Jinrihoe, founded by Chŭngsan's follower, and Reverend Sunmyung Moon's Unification Church. Of these, the former received a great deal of attention because it was the only new religion after liberation that successfully established a university north of the Han River. But all of this is very recent. Within this context, we can conclude that Won Buddhism was way ahead of its time for a new religion. Having established a university long before other new religions, the foresight and authority of the order are undeniably sound. This task can only be credited to Sot'aesan's discernment and Chŏngsan's initiative in putting the plans into action.

The second most important work after the establishment of a university is the changing of the order's name to Won Buddhism. The name change occurred in 1947; the fact that no one remembers the name 'Buddhist Dharma Society' and it is only known as Won Buddhism indicates just how significant this change is. While no amount of emphasis can express its significance, as the American expression goes, let us first take a look at events that occurred in the order during the Korean War.

The Korean War was a critical period in which many things happened; we cannot discuss all of them in this book. Of these,

Chŏngsan's interpretation of the Korean War grabs our attention. When he heard that war had broken out, Chŏngsan immediately countered, "The deep-rooted grudge between the nobles and commoners has exploded." While it is an expected response for a religious leader, the interpretation itself sounds much more like Chŭngsan than Won Buddhism. Chŭngsan once said that the souls of those who died unjust deaths went inside a bomb, and were appeased when the bomb exploded. The fact that the outbreak of the war was interpreted by the appeasement of restless souls seems to echo Chŭngsan, suggesting the extent to which Chŏngsan was influenced by Chŭngsan in the past.

Perhaps the most troublesome aspect of the Korean War was the classification of people as either right-wing or left-wing. It was the order of the day to accuse each other of being right or left, McCarthy-style, which often ended in 'kill or be killed.' Those who had the most difficult time were the leaders of any type of organization, large or small. Aligning oneself with the wrong side could be the death knell for the entire group. Chŏngsan once again demonstrated wisdom in dealing with the crisis. The plan that he presented his disciples was a highly useful one. The plan was to "not be swept up by the current of the times while avoiding senseless insubordination, and pretend to obey while avoiding responsibility." It was the perfect way to navigate Won Buddhism through the chaos of the times. While such worldly wisdom may seem too cowardly, toeing the line between avoiding clashes with the large powers and self-preservation was the best and only way to come out of the situation intact. Perhaps this was why although there was talk among the North Korean troops as they were pulling out to burn down Won Buddhist headquarters, it was given up on the grounds that the building "did not look too 'bourgeoisie.'"

The next event is another of the most important events in Won Buddhist history: the compilation of *Taejonggyŏng*, a collection of Sot'aesan's teachings. After the founding leader dies, it is customary for the second leader to oversee the compilation of the previous leader's words and teachings into scripture. Needless to say, Chŏngsan took over this role. Beginning in 1956, the completion of *Taejonggyŏng* took six years. This and *Chŏngjŏn*, Sot'aesan's work, were combined to become The Scriptures of Won Buddhism, which was published in 1962. Just as Sot'aesan did not live to see the publication of *Chŏngjŏn*, *Taejonggyŏng* was published right after Chŏngsan's death. The editing and publication of *Chŏngjŏn* was probably Chŏngsan's most significant accomplishment. This is because as long as people have records of the founder's (Sot'aesan's) teachings, the religion is able to continue. Perhaps this was why Chŏngsan devoted his later years to the editing of this scripture. Just before his death, Chŏngsan gives his trademark sermon on the Ethics of a Triple Identity (Samdong Yunri). Before we take a closer look at this sermon, I would like to share a story of the meeting between Chŏngsan and Korean poet Ŭn Ko, who has been nominated for the Nobel Prize in Literature a number of times.

It is not clear exactly when this meeting occurred. Ko—who was a Buddhist monk at the time—was permitted to meet Chŏngsan through a mutual acquaintance. What Ko said to Chŏngsan on this occasion is worth remembering. According to Won Buddhist records, Ko was taken aback by Chŏngsan's appearance. Ko declared that he had not been this shocked by anyone since his first meeting with his teacher, Hyobong. Let's go directly to Ko's reflections on the incident:

> "He looked like a full moon under a magnifying glass. His smile was perfectly harmonious with the universe without a single breach. The few words he spoke were the highest form of music... Of all paintings of mountain sages, he looked like a seated picture of the most beautiful of them. Having overcome the one-dimensionality of all past priests, he exuded a fully rounded appearance."[9]

In short, it is the highest compliment. The most interesting aspect of the above description is the part that compares Chŏngsan to a mountain sage. Looking at an image of Chŏngsan confirms the truth of this statement.

A face tells the story of its owner. It is especially easy to see in a person's face the caliber of his or her soul. While it may be possible for anyone to speak glibly with polished words, a face reveals who the person truly is on the inside. This is probably the reason behind the common Korean saying, "A person acts the way he looks." A Buddhist monk I once met said that "a face is a punishment from heaven," meaning that a face never lies. Someone whose face oozes oil with sinister looking acts exactly in this way. In terms of faces, I myself have never met an exception to this rule. This is the importance of what a face reveals. One university professor described Chŏngsan's face in the following way: "Chŏngsan's face is the most beautiful Korean face I have ever seen." Thus, we can see that Chŏngsan's face was extraordinary from the beginning.

We are approaching the end of our discussion on Chŏngsan. One year before his death, he gave a sermon that has since become his trademark. As mentioned before, it is impossible to overlook the Ethics of a Triple Identity sermon when speaking of Chŏngsan.

---

9 Yongduk Park, *In the Footsteps of Prime Dharma Master Chŏngsan*, Vol. 1 (Won Buddhism Press, 2003), 205.

I will conclude our study of him with a discussion of this famous sermon.

As the word '*samdong*' suggests, there are three ('*sam*' means 'three' in Korean) principles of *taedong*. In Confucianism, *taedong* describes the ideal society. Thus, Samdong Yunri refers to the three morals that human beings need in order to build a perfect society. The first is '*tongwon dori*,' which has to do with religion. According to this moral, all religions are actually one. Won Buddhism emphasized from Sot'aesan's day that all religions come from the same root; indeed, an entire doctrine is devoted to the United Religions movement. Won Buddhism is today the religion that most actively promotes dialogue between religions in Korea. This is due to the beliefs of its founders. However, Won Buddhism is not the only religion involved in the United Religions movement; the famous Unification Church was an early supporter. One might ask why new religions are so deeply interested in things like the United Religions movement. This is probably because new religions adhere to doctrine that runs counter to that of established religions. In response to established religions that insist on exclusive validity, new religions have suggested regarding all religions as one and opening up dialogue between religions. This is why new religions are classified as counter culture.

While I agree that all religions have the same root, I cannot agree that all of its components are the same because there are too many significant differences in detail. What I have concluded in the process of studying religion is that "religions are too similar to say they are different and too different to say they are similar." While I was involved in the inter-religious dialogue movement, I often met Won Buddhist leaders who insisted that all religions are one, solely based on what Sot'aesan said. However, how would we then explain the conflict between religions like Buddhism that do not care about the existence of God and monotheistic religions like Christianity and Islam? Through this, we can see that religions have completely different approaches to ultimate questions. Thus, we should be extremely cautious about concluding that all religions are alike. On the other hand, Chŏngsan's argument is much more logical. He argues that not only should all religions realize they are part of the same large family, but they should also work toward the realization of an ideal society (world of Il-won).

There is a great deal that can be said about the intra-religious dialogue and United Religions movements, but because this would greatly complicate our current discussion, I will instead move onto the next principle. The second moral is *dongki yŏngye*, which is a rather strange name. '*Gye*' means 'to tie up.' If the first moral was about religion, the second moral states that all people in the world are brothers and sisters because they share the same vital energy. In this way, everyone living in this world is encouraged to stop fighting amongst themselves and together form a new (Il-won) society. The concept of 'same vital energy' does not apply only to human beings. Its boundaries can be expanded to include all sentient beings. All living things are connected to one another by an energy that flows through a tightly established hierarchy. In this way, all living beings become one.

The last moral is *tongchŏk saŏp*. Both '*tonggye*' and '*tongchŏk*' are not listed in the dictionary. This is because they are both terms that were invented by Chŏngsan. Innovative philosophers often create many of their own words in the process of forming their thoughts. The Chinese character for '*chŏk*' means 'to open' or 'to reveal.'[10] To present a simplified version, this moral states that all

10 Just as all Romance languages are based on the Greek and Roman system, the basis

incidents and events in the world occur in order to achieve the goal of the Il-won world, an ideal world. This explains the term '*dongchŏk*' ('*dong*' means 'same'). In other words, this calls for everyone to focus on the same goal of creating a new society. According to this precept, anyone doing anything in any location in the world must distinguish whether or not that work makes this world a better or worse place to live. Everything in one's life contributes toward the creation of an ideal world.

Chŏngsan did not rely solely on difficult Chinese character-based words when expressing his ideas the way an old-fashioned philosopher may have done. He also states these three principles in easily understood Korean. "With Unitary truth as within a single fence, as with one family within one household, as with co-workers at a single worksite, let us construct the world as a Unitary circle." The difficult-sounding Chinese characters have been converted into understandable words. His ability to express his thoughts in simply yet profound words proves that Chŏngsan was a great philosopher. There is even no need for further explanation because the words are so easy to understand. After Sot'aesan's *Il-Won-Sang* Transmission Verse, these three principles are considered the second most important concepts in Won Buddhism.[11] However, these two transmission verses are clearly different. Sot'aesan discusses principles related to truth itself, like being, non-being and nothingness. In comparison, Chŏngsan uses these principles to describe the formation of a new world. It is the combination of theory and practice, a perfectly complementary relationship between teacher and disciple.

---

of the Korean language is Chinese. Thus, over 70% of Korean words are based on Chinese characters.

11 "Being into nonbeing and nonbeing into being, turning and turning—in the ultimate, being and nonbeing are both void, yet this void is also complete."

Chŏngsan: The Peter of Won Buddhism

Chŏngsan dies in January 1962 at the age of 63, one year after presenting this transmission verse. Both Sot'aesan and Chŏngsan die at a relatively young age, the reason for which remains unclear. In the case of Chŏngsan, he must have decided at some point that the order was now able to function without him. Having decided this, he simply left everything in the hands of his disciples, feeling free to retire from the world. The combination of the first and second leaders of Won Buddhism was a very harmonious one. Sot'aesan exercised a fatherly authority in establishing the foundations of the religion, while Chŏngsan was the benevolent mother solidified the order in ethics and morals. Both aspects are essential components of any religion, but for most cases at least one quality is found lacking, which shakes the foundations of the order after the founder has died. In comparison, Won Buddhism was established and fortified very smoothly. All of this was possible because of Chŏngsan. In this sense, Sot'aesan was very fortunate in terms of disciples. For his part, Chŏngsan's life was made significant because of Sot'aesan, having learned Sot'aesan's dharma and devoted his entire life to spreading Sot'aesan's teachings. Just like Buddha had Kasyapa, Confucius had An and Jesus had Peter (or Paul), Sot'aesan had Chŏngsan. We have now finished studying the lives of Sot'aesan and Chŏngsan, the two pillars of Won Buddhism. It is now time to take a closer look at the teachings of these two leaders.

Chapter 3

Doctrine of Won Buddhism

This chapter will focus on the content of Sot'aesan's teachings. In many ways, his teachings are highly unique. As mentioned in the previous chapter, Sot'aesan himself drafted the central tenets of Won Buddhism. Of course, the scripture that he thus produced was published posthumously, but it is the same as if this was done by Sot'aesan himself because the ideas are entirely his. *Chŏngjŏn* is not a very thick book. However, because it is so efficiently structured and organized, it is like a self-study reader for anyone who wishes to take a step closer to enlightenment himself or herself without a teacher. There is even a convenient one-page doctrinal chart which summarizes the most essential concepts of Won Buddhism. Sot'aesan seems to have gone through countless drafts in his quest to find the easiest explanation of his doctrines, a reflection of his bodhisattva-like compassion for ordinary people. Thus, it is relatively easy to introduce Won Buddhist doctrine

The Doctrinal Chart

Awareness of Grace and Requital of Grace

The Gateway of Faith Based on Retribution and Response of Cause and Effect

The Fourfold Grace

- The Grace of Heaven and Earth
- The Grace of Parents
- The Grace of Fellow Beings
- The Grace of Laws

The Four Essentials

- Developing Self-Power
- The Primacy of the Wise
- Educating Others' Children
- Venerating the Public-Spirited

Requiting Grace is a Buddha Offering

- Everywhere a Buddha Image
- Every Act a Buddha Offering

Selfless Service to the Public

Il-Won (One Circle) is
the Dharmakāya Buddha,
the original source of all
things in the universe,
the mind-seal
of all the buddhas
and sages,
and the original nature
of all sentient beings.

Transmission Verse

Being into nonbeing
and nonbeing into being,
Turning and turning-in the
ultimate,
Being and nonbeing
are both void,
Yet this void is
also complete.

Right Enlightenment and Right Practice

The Gateway of Practice Based on True Voidness and Marvelous Existence

The Threefold Study

- Cultivating the Spirit
- Inquiry into Human Affairs and
- Universal Principles
- Choice in Action

The Eight Articles

- Belief
- Zeal
- Questioning
- Dedication
- Unbelief
- Greed
- Laziness
- Foolishness

Unremitting Sŏn in Action and Rest

- Timeless *Sŏn*
- Placeless *Sŏn*

Practical Application of the Buddhadharma

because all that needs to be studied is this single volume, which is what will be done in this book.

Sot'aesan's teachings are quite different from that of most Buddhist philosophers. The vast majority of Buddhist philosophers have little interest in society because achieving their own enlightenment is a bigger priority. However, Sot'aesan's teachings emphasize a just society as much as individual enlightenment; instructions for society take up a considerable percentage of his teachings. Furthermore, the subject of Sot'aesan's first sermon was not how to become enlightened but "how the strong and the weak may evolve," an indication that Sot'aesan was deeply interested in the creation of a stable society.

This book will attempt to analyze Sot'aesan's teachings from two perspectives: individual training and the formation of a just society. Both of these aspects are explained in detail in *Chŏngjŏn*, but we will not follow its sequential order. This is because while *Chŏngjŏn* does have a well-organized structure, it may be difficult for general readers to follow it in its entirety. We will begin with individual training, but before that I will first introduce the Won Buddhist motto ("With this Great Opening of matter, let there be a Great Opening of spirit") that was created at the religion's inception. It is a fitting way to begin our journey into Won Buddhist doctrine.

"With this Great Opening of matter, let there be a Great Opening of spirit"

While Won Buddhism may have the term 'Buddhism' in its name, it is actually quite different from Buddhism per se. This can be seen even in the religion's motto. Buddha's first sermon is later transformed into the doctrine of the Four Noble Truths, the first of which states that 'life is suffering,' a highly private matter. For Buddha, the dawn of a new era was not very significant or noteworthy; his main concern was to escape—entering nirvana—from this pain-filled world. In comparison, Sot'aesan's first public statement was about the coming of a new era.

In this sense, Won Buddhism is no doubt a new religion. Interestingly, it is difficult to find in all of Won Buddhist doctrine anything that resembles the Indian Buddhist doctrine 'life is suffering.' Instead of suffering, there are many positive references to truth as a perfectly balanced circle. As Buddhism came to China, many of the pessimistic tones of its Indian counterpart were dropped; this tendency prevails in Won Buddhism as well. The most important tenet of Indian Buddhism is selflessness, but in the most Chinese version—Zen Buddhism—there is no such doctrine. Instead, focus is placed on the much more positive goal of finding the true self.

Sot'aesan's diagnosis of the world

When discussing the present era, Won Buddhism considers an awakening of spirit to be just as important as the awakening of matter. I have always argued that the central tenet of all Korean new religions, beginning with Tonghak, is the idea of the "Great awakening." Won Buddhism, also a new religion, used the term 'Awakening' in its motto. The awakening of matter is relatively easy to understand. Human society was forever changed by the development of science and industry; a world of great awakening had truly been formed. Never since the dawn of human history has technology developed at such a rapid pace. However, our spiritual state is unable to keep up. We should be able to govern and control matter, but instead we are the ones being controlled like slaves. Sot'aesan had a very befitting analogy for the current state of humanity: a child with a knife in his hand. The parallel could not have been more appropriate.

Firstly, humanity is compared to a child. As a whole, humanity is no more than ten years old. The wars in Afghanistan and Iraq resemble the petty fights of children who all want the biggest piece of pie. The only difference is in scale: the basic goal of taking as much of the other's possessions as possible is the same. The difference between an adult and a child is that an adult has the ability to understand a situation from someone else's perspective. Most adults know that when something goes wrong between two people, both parties are at fault rather than only one. However, children are not aware of this. For children, fault is never found in oneself but always in others. Blaming someone else is a childish level of thought. When observing the world today, it is difficult to find a national leader who is willing to acknowledge wrongdoing and take responsibility. Just as with children, it is usually the other person's fault. This shows that the world's mental age is stuck at the level of a child.

This was not a problem for humanity in the past, because nobody had much of anything worth fighting over. The only tools that people had in hand were things like the knife, shovel or plow. These were not too harmful to the environment. The situation today has completely changed. Instead of the primitive tools of antiquity, people now have excavators and explosives that can destroy the environment with the press of a button. The result is that, for the first time in human history, people are living in an era in which self-destruction is a very real possibility. From the earth's perspective, there was probably never a time that one species wreaked so much havoc on the planet. In this sense, human beings are like parasites, because destruction always follows wherever humans go. Forests that had existed for several hundred million years were chopped down for no other reason than the greed of people who wanted more money. The death of nature also means the death of all life forms. But because there is no place on the planet that is untouched by human beings, the environmental problem becomes more critical.

Questions remain as to whether this motto was really referring to environmental damage. Sot'aesan never explicitly stated that the environmental problem would become more serious. But his prophesy about the child holding a knife seems to predict environmental disaster. The many tools and devices that have been created thanks to the development of science can improve the quality of our lives, but they also have the power to bring about large-scale destruction like what is happening to our environment today. The same logic applies to a knife. It is a necessity in cooking but can also be used as a murder weapon. Sot'aesan believed that modern civilization is much like this knife. Notwithstanding spilt milk, what can we do to at least make amends? Don't we need to let the child grow up? This is where the great awakening of the spirit comes in. "Great opening of the spirit" may sound strange, but it basically means that we should hurry up and become true adults.

In fact, experts agree that our environmental problems can only be solved by cutting current consumption levels (especially of developed countries) by at least half. Too many products are manufactured that we do not really need. In order to maximize profit, companies produce lots of useless products to tempt consumers. In no time at all, people suddenly find themselves machines that consume endlessly without purpose: basically, consumption for the sake of consumption. As a result, the earth is covered by the garbage of these products. The amount of waste able to be accommodated by the planet was exceeded long ago, and people were gradually becoming slaves of materialism. It was as if their sole purpose for existence was to sell, buy and consume. Some say that if the entire Chinese population of over one billion consumes at the same level as South Korea, the world would self destruct. But China will continue its economic development without heeding such warnings. Chinese consumption will rise, as would the Earth's temperature; this makes for a truly gloomy situation (of course, the most urgent task is for Americans to reduce their consumption!). This is probably why Sot'aesan, who was fully aware of all this, was so focused on spiritual awakening.

The solution

Then what are we to do? Sot'aesan proposed a textbook-like solution: faith based on fundamental truth and the practice of moral living. These two concepts, which may sound pedantic, are the pillars of Sot'aesan's teachings. To make future explanations easier, let us look at the simplified version. Why did Sot'aesan place so much emphasis on fundamental truth? At its core, Sot'aesan's teachings are permeated by a strong distrust of anything related to enchantment or faith based on the seeking of personal fortune. Sot'aesan disapproved of highly spiritual people devoting themselves to worshipping inanimate objects like Buddha statues or praying to rocks at village shrines for fortune. This was all due to an 'inverted' worldview. In other words, it was something reminiscent of the old pre-awakening era. Sot'aesan firmly believed that once people realized their true worth, they would be able to free themselves from such 'superstitious' practices.

According to Sot'aesan, there was no longer any reason to take a circumlocutory path to truth because there was a more direct path available. Sot'aesan proposed the circle as a close-up method for experiencing truth. This is the famous *Il-Won-Sang*. The circle is the most 'truth-like' symbol, which was quite a revolutionary concept for the day. This is why when drawing a *mandala*, the Buddhist symbol for enlightenment, the most frequently used shape is a circle. Sot'aesan argued that one would attain enlightenment by uniting one's mind with the circle, not by praying to a man-made Buddha statue. He had utmost confidence in the fact that the *Il-Won-Sang* is truth. We will look more closely at the *Il-Won-Sang* in a later section.

Once you become this close to truth, the method of practice changes as well. Traditional Buddhism placed too much emphasis on the prerequisite of having to leave the secular world behind. Sot'aesan did not approve of this practice because in his eyes, it was a teaching slanted too much toward one side. A truly great teaching should be able to be practiced within the boundaries of everyday life. Sot'aesan called this the "training of realistic ethics." Instead of going into the mountains to train and living the rest of one's life without any purpose, one should live as a hardworking member of society as well as train. This is summarized by the motto "dharma as life." Sot'aesan advises us to perform every task encountered in daily life as if it were a Buddha offering. This is "Every act a Buddha offering." Going to a temple to pray to a Buddha statue ceases to be a Buddha offering. In fact, it then becomes an anti-offering: the alienation of the practice of Buddha offering. All who are training must approach everything in life as if it were a Buddha offering and try their best to prepare their minds. Thus, by circular logic, everything becomes a Buddha offering because there is no place without a Buddha image. This is the motto "everywhere a Buddha image." From this perspective, it is only natural to conclude that a Buddha statue trapped inside a temple is nothing more than superstition.

The focus is not on just Buddha offering. Although of course it is important to treat all things as Buddha, one must not forget personal training. Daily life must become indistinguishable from training. In traditional Buddhism, one cannot train and perform daily chores at the same time, and secular convention dictates that training cannot be done while living with one's parents or wife and children. This is why in the past, one had to leave one's family and physically go away from home in order to train. Sot'aesan argued that study and work are the same; good performance in one automatically means good performance in the other. This is considered to be true 'study,' or Timeless Sŏn and Placeless Sŏn (Sŏn means Zen here). Real training can be done any time and in any place. While this is easy enough to say, it is actually a very difficult level to be reached. But it must be done, because it is the correct path.

According to Sot'aesan, sŏn that is performed in quiet places is 'diseased sŏn.' This type of training, like a mushroom removed from the shade, loses its power when placed in an entirely different situation—i.e. a noisy marketplace—and is not true training. Also, a Way that can only be achieved by a select group of people is only a minor Way at best. The true Way is one that can be achieved by anyone. Training done by only a few people in remote locations—inside the mountains or a temple—does not properly reflect a Great Awakening, because anyone should be able to train anywhere. Class distinctions disappear and an awareness of equity takes its place. In the past, only a few monks could train; Sot'aesan rejected this idea.

Every act a Buddha offering, everywhere a Buddha image, timeless sŏn and placeless sŏn are central tenets of Won Buddhism that can be found at the bottom of the doctrinal chart. Once the proper method of training is learned, the trainee's awareness becomes brighter and gradually changes into a person befitting of the Great Awakening era. His body becomes stronger and he grows more spiritually mature. In other words, the trainee acquires an awakened disposition. One must have reached this level in order to remain unswayed by the development of science or material civilization. In Won Buddhism, this state is known as 'wholeness of both spirit and flesh,' the goal that all believers hope to reach.

Let us now take a look at how Won Buddhists train and what kind of society they aspire toward in order to reach this goal.

How should we train? – Personal practice

Chŏngjŏn presents a detailed guide on how to do personal practice. However, we will not follow the order of *Chŏngjŏn* because its structure can seem boring to the average reader. This can be dealt with on a more in-depth level in an academic paper; for our purposes, let us look at Sot'aesan's teachings in a way that is easy for lay readers to understand. The central text will be *Chŏngjŏn*, but direct quotations will also be taken from *Taejonggyŏng*, the collection of Sot'aesan's maxims.

Which topic should be looked at first? I believe that religion and everything related to it begins with repentance. This is why Jesus declared "Repent, for the kingdom of heaven is near." Furthermore, when doing mental training or meditation, the first thoughts to come to mind are not about the *koan* at hand but reflection on one's life. It is only after this self-reflection has continued for some time that one is finally able to focus on the *koan*. This is probably because the body and mind must be cleaned out to a certain extent before proper training can take place. It is unclear whether Sot'aesan actually thought this way about repentance, but let us begin with these assumptions.

Repentance and the keeping of precepts

True Repentance

Sot'aesan also believed that repentance was the starting point of religious life. He once said that repentance is "the first step in abandoning one's old life and opening oneself to cultivating a new life, and the initial gateway for setting aside evil ways and entering into good ways." His opinion on sin and *karma* also reflects heavy influence from Buddhism. Because sin originates in the heart, this would disappear if the heart's function is 'turned off.' On the other hand, *karma*, which makes reincarnation possible, is similar to ignorance. Once the truth is realized, this *karma* can be thrown off in an instant—the way turning on a light even after eons of darkness dispels the dark. Then how must one repent? Sot'aesan's answer to this question reflects his wisdom as well as his ability to compose good analogies.

People often make the mistake of thinking that to repent

simply means regretting one's past wrongdoings. But this is only a short-term definition. Temporary repentance may bring some fortune, but it is only a band-aid solution because sin will continue to occur if it is not rooted out entirely. Then, what is the root cause of sin? As seen previously, sin in Buddhism is caused by the three evils of greed, hatred and delusion. Thus, repenting only one's day-to-day sins while not addressing the three evils is absolutely useless. Sot'aesan illustrates this with a very simple analogy. He compared repenting only one's daily sins without regard for the three evils to trying to reduce the temperature of water boiling in a cauldron by pouring a little bit of cold water into it while doing nothing about the burning firewood underneath. The point here is that leaving the fire burning will make all other attempts to reduce temperature useless.

The boiling water probably symbolizes earthly passions. I believe that this analogy is an especially befitting one. At large-scale revivals, there are often people who cry out in repentance of their past. But according to Sot'aesan, all of this is a waste of time. For him, there is no use in seeking forgiveness for one's sins while leaving its root deep inside the heart untouched. He often remarked that although many repent of past sins, few of them do not commit those same errors again.

On the other hand, this is not to say that repentance for individual sins has no effect at all. Sot'aesan, like the benevolent philosopher that he was, never entirely eliminated anything. He called it by its Won Buddhist term, 'repentance by action.' The Chinese characters that spell this term literally mean 'repenting for each single action.' Sins committed each day were to be confessed before the Three Jewels of Buddhism (Buddha, Dharma, and Sangha) along with a promise to do good deeds. Of course, repentance by action cannot substitute for complete repentance. The latter requires the fixing of fundamental wrongs, a process akin to surgery. Sot'aesan called this 'repentance by principle,' a concept which is based on the principle that the nature of transgressions is void. Buddhism teaches that everything in the world is void: sin is no exception to this rule. As such, both types of repentance are needed to complete the process. To apply this to the 'cooling of boiling water' analogy, cold water would be poured into the cauldron while the fire is being put out (of the two, the latter is much more important). In this way, all sin regardless of degree can be eliminated.

Precepts to guard the heart

During or directly after repentance, one thing that must be done is the keeping of precepts. Most people are turned off by the mere mention of the word 'religion.' This is usually because of precepts and the fact that they restrict one's life by forbidding certain things, often worded as 'do not do such and such.' But precepts are not to be taken lightly. While one should not deify precepts or become overly attached to them, they cannot simply be written off either. Precepts exist in order to protect a believer when he or she is not yet firmly established in faith. For example, children need to be told "do not touch the hot oven" or "do not touch knives" for their own protection. But it cannot be explained to very small children why they must not do such things. This is because they would not understand even if they were told. The same applies for religious precepts. It may not be possible in the early stage for believers to understand why they must obey certain rules. But precepts are crucial especially in the early stages of faith because they are what protect the still-fragile faith of new believers.

Once the level of training or wisdom increases, precepts are no longer necessary. As one's faith becomes more firmly entrenched, he or she will act within the boundary of the precepts without having to be reminded of them.

Sot'aesan's prescription for precepts is a highly pragmatic one which once again speaks to his character and generosity. Sot'aesan created three grades of precepts; there are several interesting aspects of the precepts for beginners—called 'ordinary grade'—that I would like to point out. These show that Sot'aesan was very much a rational thinker. There is no significant difference between the ten precepts for beginners and those for other grades. Among other things, they prevent killing, stealing and sexual misconduct and encourage believers to refrain from smoking. The interesting part is the phrase "without due cause" that is attached to the end of several of the precepts. For example, one states "do not consume intoxicants without due cause." This means that rather than a command to not drink at all, the rule of thumb is to not drink without good reason. In other words, things like robbery or sexual misconduct are banned entirely because these are undesirable under any circumstances, but other things like killing living things, drinking alcohol ('intoxicants'), arguing ('fighting'), exchanging of money and smoking are not entirely prohibited but permitted when circumstances call for them. These are especially logical when considering that as a functioning member of society, it is impossible to avoid some of the above precepts. There are instances when drinking, smoking or arguing for the common good is inevitable. While this may not be appropriate for those in the priesthood, the same standard cannot be held to lay believers. For example, it would be like telling a fisherman that he should not kill living things, effectively meaning that he should give up his profession and thus have no way to make a living. In this type of case, there is clearly a due cause. But Sot'aesan advises that even in this case, one must not become too insensitive to the catching of fish and always have a repentant heart concerning it.

While we are on the subject of animal flesh, I would like to point out that Won Buddhism does not prevent its ministers from eating meat. Sot'aesan, displaying his logical prowess even in this case, said that while eating meat should be refrained from if possible, if it must be eaten then it is better to avoid four-legged mammals and choose things like fish or other creatures further down on the food chain (this story is told often within the order). In technical terms, he was recommending less sentient animals. Also, smoking and drinking are not entirely forbidden to ministers but as a rule these are usually avoided (from what I know, alcohol is permitted on occasion but almost all do not smoke). Sot'aesan once succeeded in persuading someone who was new to the faith to completely give up smoking and drinking. He would point out to his disciples that one does not die from avoiding smoking and drinking, thus encouraging their voluntary participation in keeping the precepts. I have not yet seen any instance in which Sot'aesan resorted to extremes to get something done. There are other precepts as well, but I will not cover these as most are commonly found in other religions as well.

One aspect of Sot'aesan's message concerning repentance and precepts deserves some attention. He harshly rebukes the many so-called ascetics of his day who engaged in all sorts of unconstrained acts; many such cases are found in Buddhism as well. There are monks who enjoy meat and alcohol without restraint—the same goes for their interaction with women—and justify all of this as a method of salvation for the unenlightened. When criticized for the impropriety of their actions, they insist that you must not think in such a narrow-minded manner. To such people, I always say that "if you wanted to do such things, you should not have entered the priesthood to begin with. Once you are in, you must keep the precepts."

There are many opinions about the keeping of precepts, but of these I believe that Sot'aesan's critique is the most reasonable. According to him, people like those mentioned above who do not keep precepts "realize only that the self-nature is free from discrimination, but do not realize that it also involves discriminations." What did Sot'aesan mean by this? While this may be a bit difficult for general readers to understand, the most basic doctrine of Buddhism states that the purest consciousness that lies deep within our hearts—it can be called Buddha nature or divine nature—transcends dualistic distinctions like good and evil, large and small, and ugly and beautiful. However, this does not mean that self-nature is unable to distinguish between right and wrong. This is especially important in daily life, where if things are not kept distinguished it may lead to societal chaos as in the case of "your husband is my husband and my husband is your husband," according to the non duality theory. Thus, self-nature has the ability to both discriminate as well as not discriminate. Again, this is a rather difficult concept. Let us move on.

The next explanation is also noteworthy. Sot'aesan sounds the warning bell for those who, after having completed their beginner's training, believe that they are done for good and no longer do repentance or training. Sot'aesan's teaching that one must continue to train even after having achieved enlightenment is unique in many ways. This means that being enlightened does not eliminate all earthly sins at once. However, requiring enlightened people to continue to repent brings up the question of whether enlightened people continue to sin. Ramakrishna, the most eminent yogi of nineteenth century India, also once said that even those who have met Brahman can still have sins left. This is like how even after a leaf has fallen off, a mark remains on the branch. There is apparently no end to training.

Things to do while keeping precepts

In most religions, one can find precepts saying 'do not do such and such' paired with more positive commands like 'do such and such.' This duality is found in Confucianism in the active precept of faithfulness and the passive precept of moral reciprocity. The same goes for Christianity. In Christianity, if the Ten Commandments are passive precepts meant to control human conduct, Jesus' teaching to "love your neighbors" is an active precept (Jesus himself did not deny the need for off-limits areas, but taught that these are to be transcended). The same is found in Won Buddhism. The precepts are followed by a chapter entitled 'Essential Discourse on Commanding the Nature;' this can be seen as the active precept. This chapter presents rules to abide by in order to guide ourselves along the right path; it emphasizes things that should be done rather than saying 'do not do such and such' and forbidding things that should not be done. There are sixteen items total, including "Believe not in the person alone, but in the dharma," "Having been born as humans among all the four types of birth, we should have a love of learning" and "When responding to any matter, maintain a respectful state of mind and fear the rise of covetous greed as if it were a lion."

Interestingly, the tenth item states that "should you learn of another's fault, do not reveal it but use it instead to perceive your own faults." In other words, lessons learned from someone else's faults should be kept to oneself and not be displayed for everyone else's edification. While this may seem strange at first, it actually reflects the virtue of tolerance for others, a very important aspect of religion. When someone does something wrong, we usually point this out to him or her and request that it be fixed. But people normally do not respond well to criticism and try to resist it. To avoid this type of situation, a person must do his best to realize his own mistakes.

Sot'aesan once told the following story: when one of Buddha's disciples committed a wrongdoing, he would not criticize the disciple for it directly but stand next to him and do the exact same thing. In this way, Buddha wanted the disciple to learn for himself that his actions were wrong. I believe that this method of pointing out errors is what 'humane' education is all about; the method preserves the person's dignity while allowing him to see his faults and correct them. In this sense, the self-criticism that was a hallmark of the communist movement in many countries may look just fine. However, it is actually a very inhumane device because it forcibly reveals the faults of the individual in front of the group. People are more receptive to a kind word than this type of point-blank criticism.

The next point that we will go over briefly is the seventh one: "When responding to any matter, maintain a respectful state of mind." It may be unclear what 'having respect for an object' means, but Sot'aesan explains this with a concrete example. Maintaining a respectful state of mind for objects does not mean idolatry but to exercise caution in all things. If a person is caught stealing a match by the owner of the store, he will be subject to a lot of ridicule and embarrassment. Depending on the situation, he could even have to serve a prison sentence. All of this is a result of having lost respect for an object: the match. Sot'aesan says that if even a humble match deserves a certain amount of respect, even more would be required for a greater object or a human being. If this level of respect is maintained for all things, I can have the entire world in the palm of my hand, but thoughtless disregard only brings harm.

How to train

We have now covered all the basics required for training. The purpose of Won Buddhism is to become enlightened through training; therefore, it is one of the pillars of Won Buddhist doctrine. Sot'aesan's method of training is outlined very systematically. The broadest categorization is time: there is fixed-term training, which is done at set times throughout the year, and daily training, which is done every day. Examples of the former are the dharma of reciting Buddha's name and dharma of seated meditation. It is explained in great detail in the scripture and we will also be covering this thoroughly. Fixed-term training is done while sitting quietly, and daily training is done within the hectic routine of daily life. The section on daily training gives tips for how to train in daily life by using bits of free time and how to train after eating dinner. It also explains in detail what to be careful of when visiting the temple, but I leave this part out because it does not apply to general readers.

For both fixed-term training and daily training, there is one point to always keep in mind. This is what is known as the Threefold Study in Won Buddhism. The wording alone is probably not enough to have a clear idea of what this concept is: let us go over it briefly here.

Three basic attitudes for training: The Threefold Study

The term "threefold study" itself is a rather strange choice of words. The three aspects of it are: 1) cultivating the spirit, 2) inquiry into human affairs and universal principles and 3) choice in action. The terms are more difficult than they look because they are either unfamiliar or so general that this actually makes the meaning more unclear.

Let us look at the first part, cultivating the spirit. To summarize its three subheadings, human beings are different from animals in that their greed knows no end; thus, people must obtain the autonomous power required to control their minds and do training. The content of this part may seem unoriginal, but it occupies an important position in training theory.

The second attitude is inquiry into human affairs and universal principles. It states that all incidents in life can be understood by understanding the principles of everything that exists in this world. Without this, one would not know the law of cause and effect or how pain comes into existence and then dies out. To avoid being left out of the loop, one must be aware of the principles that govern the universe and the complexities of human relationships. None of the above seems very controversial or unique: let us move on.

The third part is choice of action. This states that even if one has the power of cultivation and the power from inquiry into human affairs and universal principles, it is all useless unless it is put into action. Here, 'action' implies real-life situations. Thus, it strengthens applicability. As we have just seen, there is nothing in the threefold study that is radically different or new.

Four things to keep and four things to throw away: Eight Articles

When training in the above fashion, there are things that are necessary for the process and things that must be thrown out. There are four of each of these two categories, totaling eight altogether—thus, the reason why these are called the 'eight articles.' First, the four articles to develop or the things that must be kept closely resemble what is considered important in traditional Zen Buddhism. Zen Buddhism states that we must have three qualities in order to become enlightened. These are belief, zeal and questioning, all of which are significant. Belief indicates a strong faith in oneself that 'if I practice, I will become enlightened in the end.' Without this faith, there is no way that enlightenment can be achieved. On the other hand, zeal is the anger of 'why have I not yet become enlightened' in one's efforts. By awakening one's feelings of inferiority, it becomes the fuel for a more aggressive effort. Questioning is a strong attachment to one's *koan*. If you do not feel the need to find the solution of a *koan*, there will be no progress. To summarize all three, confidence that I will become enlightened is paired with a strong devotion to *koan*, and I become angry if I do not progress as quickly as planned. Won Buddhism adds one more quality—dedication—making a total of four articles. Dedication is exactly what it sounds like: a constant and steady faith, which is also a central virtue in the Confucian text Doctrine of the Mean.

There is nothing to question about the articles we have seen thus far, but among the four articles to abandon there are potential problems. The Chinese characters used for the term 'abandon' are ones that are not commonly used, but the more pressing question is why these four articles are so negative. There is nothing unique about them: unbelief, greed, laziness and foolishness. On the doctrinal chart, these four qualities are the only negative words. One would think that a doctrinal chart should be composed of only perfect qualities; it is a mystery why these four very generic negative qualities are on this diagram at all. There is no way of knowing why Sot'aesan placed these common evils on a chart that should only contain the greatest truths. These articles do not reflect the finely tuned analysis that is present in all of Sot'aesan's other theories: this is what is so strange. Setting our doubts aside, let us move on from our theoretical discussion to more concrete teachings.

Buddhist Training: The Dharma of Reciting the Buddha's Name and The Dharma of Seated Meditation

For training, Sot'aesan discusses two pillars: the dharma of reciting the Buddha's name and the dharma of seated meditation. However, these do not seem very different from each other; rather, they seem to be complementary, which is evidence of Sot'aesan's long experience. Anyone who has ever studied Buddhism knows that there is an unstated conflict between those who recite Buddha's name and those who believe in seated meditation. The latter claim superiority over the former, mainly because believers in meditation have little regard for those who chant Buddha's name in training. According to supporters of meditation, reciting the Buddha's name is merely a substitute for those who are not persistent enough to reach truth. However, this is only a prejudice. Many religious histories have shown that reciting Buddha's name is also a good method to approach 'truth.' Perhaps this is why Sot'aesan emphasized seated meditation but also accommodated the reciting of Buddha's name.

Sot'aesan believed that both methods had their respective advantages. Simply put, reciting the Buddha's name was a good method in places with a lot of people around or times like daytime that are full of distractions. In these situations, Sot'aesan believed that reciting Buddha's name over and over again could calm the mind and thus prepare it for meditation. I have a lot of respect for this reciprocal way of management. It is only small-minded people who insist on exclusivity. On the other hand, neither Sot'aesan nor his disciple Chŏngsan ever wrote something off entirely, implying that everything in the world exists for a reason.

Sot'aesan's wise teachings did not end here. He always took into account all aspects of a situation. One day, he met a group of youth who were on their way to 'punish' a pseudo religion. Sot'aesan encouraged them, all the while reminding the youth that the pseudo religion was doing its best to improve the world albeit in a strange method. The reasoning behind this comment was that it was time for people to begin making change in earnest, and it was the responsibility of religions to awaken them. It is only after people have experienced useless activities without productivity or purpose that they would return to their senses. If this was the role of pseudo religions, what was that of the youth? Sot'aesan believed that these youth had a definite purpose—one that was much more valuable than that of the pseudo religions—of guiding the latter so that they could voluntarily admit their own mistakes and reform themselves. In this way, Sot'aesan always looked at all angles of a situation.

In this regard, Chŏngsan was no less flexible than his teacher. Let us look at his reaction to *fengshui*. Chŏngsan approved of burial fengshui because it was in line with Won Buddhism's emphasis on filial piety. However, he rejected the idea that future generations became fortunate from the energy emanating from their ancestor's bones. Chŏngsan reasoned that plants do not receive nutrients from the soil once they are dead, making it similarly impossible for the skulls of one's ancestors to have any effect either. He further pointed out that all of this was simply a way of emphasizing the importance of filial piety. We can see here that Chŏngsan's perspective is a generally positive one that attempts to see things from a logical point of view, a mature position. This stands in stark contrast with small-minded or less mature people's insistence on excluding certain things. We have wandered slightly off-track from our original discussion. Let us return to our discussion of practice.

The Means of Concentration: The Dharma of Reciting the Buddha's Name

As we have just mentioned, the dharma of reciting the Buddha's name is highly effective in gathering the mind to concentrate. Sot'aesan adapted the traditional form of this practice to suit his beliefs. If in the past people recited Amitabha Buddha's name so that its power would allow them to be reborn in paradise, Sot'aesan called for people to rise above this type of faith.[1] According to him, Amitabha Buddha was not a Buddha who was waiting somewhere in the Western paradise. Rather, he is not a being per se but our most basic persona. Sot'aesan called this 'self-nature,' which itself is enlightenment and "originally pure, utterly void of transgressions and merits, with all suffering exter-

---

1 In Buddhism there are many Buddhas other than Sakyamuni, the historic Buddha. While the latter is a historical figure who actually lived, the former is a category of Buddhas that was created for the benefit of lay believers. One of the most popular is Amitabha Buddha, who is believed to live in paradise waiting for people who have died.

nally extinguished." It is a state in which there is neither pain nor any need for punishment or reward. The focus was no longer on reciting 'Amitabha Buddha' so that one could go to paradise, but to always remember that I myself am Amitabha Buddha.

This interpretation can also be seen in traditional Buddhism. In traditional Buddhism, the most fundamental doctrine is the concept of nonduality, which means that one's heart and Amitabha Buddha are one and the same (the same goes for this world and paradise). Furthermore, the fact that paradise itself is simply a device is well-known within Buddhism. Paradise, where Amitabha Buddha lives, is said to be somewhere far away in the West. The necessity of cardinal direction itself implies that once the world expands to include outer space, it has no meaning. It is common knowledge among Buddhists that the concept of paradise was created for those who have little or no mental training. However, it is rare to see a case like Sot'aesan in which he specifically equates self-nature with Amitabha Buddha. His logical prowess again proves its worth.

Sot'aesan's pragmatic way of thinking and his deep compassion appear most strongly in the section that explains how to recite the Buddha's name. The chapter has such detailed instructions that simply reading it would make a teacher unnecessary. Among other things, it states that the body should be kept still and the chanting should be done in a tone of voice that is not too loud or soft. It also advises that one should not envision a Buddha or the splendors in paradise while chanting. While reciting the Buddha's name is meant to rid the mind of extraneous thoughts, Sot'aesan advises refraining from this if the situation is such that reciting the Buddha's name would actually increase distraction. This dharma is to be performed to calm the mind when angry or in the throes of greed. It is to be done not only in times of difficulty but also to discipline one's mind when happy. Lastly, Sot'aesan states that one who truly understands the truth of this dharma can defeat any demon by performing it.

What is the truth that Sot'aesan is referring to? What is so great about continuously reciting Buddha's name? The sole purpose of incantation is to focus the mind. Most methods of meditation are centered on the ability to concentrate, because concentration that is deep enough calms the mind and allows the person to see one's inner self. The analogy of the pearl in the mud can be applied here. The pearl represents our deepest inner self, which in Buddhism is Buddha-nature. It usually cannot be seen because it is covered by mud; only after the water becomes calm does the mud sink to the bottom and the pearl become visible. It is this function that incantation is meant to perform. Chanting brings the mind into a deeper level of concentration from which one can see self-nature.

My explanation has become too lengthy. However, Sot'aesan, like Buddha and Jesus before him, explained the merits of this dharma with a simple story. A long time ago, an uneducated peddler of straw shoes (called '*chipsin*' in Korean) wanted to cultivate himself religiously and asked an ascetic about the Way. The ascetic's response was "*chŭksim sibul*," a Chinese maxim which means 'a clear mind without predetermined thoughts is Buddha-nature.' There is a great deal that can be said about this term, but let us move on for now. This shoe peddler, who was illiterate, instead heard "*chipsin se bŏl* (which means 'three pairs of straw shoes' in Korean)." Being simple and uneducated, this peddler did not doubt what he had heard and spent several years repeating the phrase *chipsin se bŏl*. The story ends with the peddler realizing one day that his mind had opened and was one with Buddha. The moral of the story is that the content of the incantation is inconsequential. The important part is mental concentration, which is highlighted by Sot'aesan's fitting story of the shoe peddler.

'Real' Meditation: The Dharma of Seated Meditation

The dharma of seated meditation is easier than it sounds. Sot'aesan defines it to be "a method that, in the body, causes the fiery energy to descend and the watery energy to ascend." The processing point for all five senses, the brain is where heat rises up to for most people. Once other distractions like anger and greed are added to the mix, the fiery energy grows so much that meditation becomes impossible. Sot'aesan compared this waste of mental energy to the oil in a lamp becoming used up. The law of ascending water and descending fire can help control this tendency. In order to achieve this state, Sot'aesan suggests the dharma of resting in the elixir field.

Seated meditation usually brings to mind the Zen, but Sot'aesan believed that resting in the elixir field was of equal importance. Resting in the elixir field, according to Sot'aesan's definition, is the gathering of the body's energy into the elixir field and concentrating only on it. When breathing, inhaling must be strong while exhaling is short and weak. In this way, thoughts are prevented from wandering and the mind can be at peace in the elixir field. Resting in the elixir field is effective not only for seated meditation but is also hygienic. It reduces illness, improves skin complexion and recharges one's energy, which can lengthen one's lifespan.

Within traditional Buddhism, the practice of resting in the elixir field as defined by Sot'aesan is reserved for non-believers and beginners in the faith. The vast majority of Korean Buddhism is made up of conservatives who believe that *koan* Zen is the only way to reach enlightenment. I cannot agree with this because while *koan* Zen is certainly a good method, it is neither the best nor the only method available to reach enlightenment. From my experience, *koan* Zen is like winning the lottery. All is well if one happens to obtain the correct answer; if not, the entire process is a waste of time. *Koan* Zen is exactly like someone who buys a lottery ticket everyday in the hope that one of those tickets will contain the winning number. Furthermore, it is a method that may not be appropriate for the general public. Thinking too much only of one *koan* can raise the level of fiery energy, causing more stress. Thus, unless enlightenment is one's utmost priority, I cannot help thinking that Sot'aesan's dharma of resting in the elixir field may be much more practical for the lay believer.

Sot'aesan seems to have gotten wind of this early on. He argues the following in defense of the dharma of resting in the elixir field against *koan* Zen extremists, who criticized the former as 'dead Zen.' Only appropriate for a small minority, *koan* Zen is not the type of training that most people can do. Excessive concentration on one *koan* can lead to various physical ailments. Moreover, *koan* Zen is not a good method for people who doubt the power of *koan*. In comparison, one does not have to worry about this for resting in the elixir field. This teaching is not only profound but also very practical. In reality, it is not easy to want to solve a *koan*. Having this desire alone means that the trainee has made significant progress, and this occurs for only very few. The nature of this phenomena—the fact that only a small minority can properly train in *koan* Zen—implies that it cannot be applied to the general population.

Furthermore, *koan* Zen is only one training method that was developed relatively late in the process of Buddhism's development in China. The method that has been in existence throughout the history of Buddhism in India and the East as a whole is breath training, which attempts to reach deep concentration by counting each breath. It is a method that was often used by Buddha himself. There might not be any such thing as the perfect training method to reach enlightenment, but on the other hand it may be that the simplest method is the best one.

There are many complicated discussions that can be had about this topic, but I will close instead with the following story. An American youth decided to go to India and find the best teacher who would teach him how to become enlightened. The youth, who lived on the East coast, hitchhiked to California. Once he arrived in California, he worked at various odd jobs to save up enough money to go to India. After reaching India, the youth endured all kinds of difficulties and finally met the teacher he had been searching for. He was obviously very excited, confident that his dream was on the brink of coming true. The dream, of course, was that he would recite the best *mantra* and be united with Brahman through an otherworldly experience. However, the teacher's teaching was too easy. The teacher told the youth, who had traveled countless miles to meet him, to sit facing the wall in lotus position and focus on his breathing. That was all, something that could easily have been done right in New York City. The ending of this story is rather deflating, but in a sense it is an obvious one. The moral is that meditation requires nothing else but to concentrate and calm the mind. I wonder whether it was not for this reason that Sot'aesan recommended the dharma of resting in the elixir field.

In addition, Sot'aesan's instructions on seated meditation are outlined in great detail over nine steps. For first-time trainees, Sot'aesan warns that the cross-legged position may be painful for the legs and that the trainee may suffer from delusions. After outlining various possible difficulties, he then offers solutions for them: the position of the legs can be re-adjusted and the delusions should simply be acknowledged for what they are, after which they will eventually disappear. The explanation carefully and considerately points out all possible points. Sot'aesan also even adds that the trainee may feel like one's entire body is covered by crawling ants, in which case it is important not to scratch the area that itches. He warns against forming an image or 'idol' in one's mind during meditation, and concludes that these are to be ignored even if they do materialize. All of this is content that Buddhists are well acquainted with, but in all of my reading and research I have not found a scripture that outlines these principles in such simple and easily understood language.

Then what happens after one has trained in this way? Let us look at Sot'aesan's exact words: "You ultimately will forget the distinction between self and others and will forget time and place and, resting in the genuine realm of consummate quiescence and nondiscriminations, you will rejoice in an unparalleled bliss of mind." This basically means that the self is forgotten and one enters an enlightened state of great happiness. Having never been anywhere near enlightenment, I have no experience to draw any conclusions from. However, those who have reached that state all agree that it is a feeling of boundless joy. Ramakrishna, the greatest yogi of nineteenth century India, noted that enlightenment (for men) brings happiness that cannot be compared to the pleasure of lying with a woman. This state is known as supreme bliss.

The above discussion may lead to the incorrect conclusion that Sot'aesan did not consider *koan* Zen to be important. This was not the case at all. Having faith in the effectiveness of *koan* Zen, Sot'aesan lists twenty *koans* for trainees to meditate on. The *koans* that Sot'aesan believed to be the most effective are not ones that give strange answers to common questions but can make anyone curious after having thought about it in a logical manner. For example, Sot'aesan does not include *koan* like "what is Buddhadharma," a commonly used *koan* in traditional Buddhism for which the answer is something bizarre like "shit stick" or "pine tree in the front yard." Instead, they ask things like "Buddha never spoke a single dharma in his lifetime. What does this mean?," "When a person is in a deep, dreamless sleep, where is the numinous awareness that makes one sentient?," "Are all things in the universe subject to arising and ceasing or free from arising and ceasing?" and "The numinous awareness of people who attain nirvana is merged with the Dharmakaya. How, then, do individual spirits become divided again?" It would be difficult to ponder the answer to a question like "Why did Zhaozhou say that a dog does not have Buddha-nature?," a *koan* found in traditional Buddhism. Perhaps this is what Sot'aesan hoped to avoid by only choosing *koan* for which logical answers can be found.

Sot'aesan's ideal method of meditation is a balanced combination of both *koan* Zen and breath meditation. Because most people are unable to completely focus on wanting to find the answer to a *koan*, he proposed that time be spent separately on both breath meditation and *koan*. In this way, one would obtain tranquility from breath meditation and wisdom from *koan* Zen, which would then prevent both useless emptiness and the tendency to argue without discernment. This is the Wholeness of both

Tranquilness and Wisdom. Thus, Sot'aesan's answer is highly logical, but traditional Buddhists who insist on *koan* Zen may object to the idea. They point out that it is difficult enough to arrive at the answer even when meditating on *koan* night and day; the dividing of time so that *koan* meditation is only done for set hours during the day seems doubtful at best. They certainly have a point. However, one must not ignore the potential abuses of *koan* Zen. One priest is said to have focused on one *koan* for so long that he became ill and his head burst out bleeding. A psychiatrist once noted that after the seasonal fixed training periods, monks seek medical help because their brains have become overheated from their exertions. All of this goes to show that there are no few problems related to *koan* Zen.

The Flower of Seated Meditation

After having meditated in this fashion, it is then time to reach the highest state. Sot'aesan called it 'timeless Zen,' which basically means 'practicing Zen meditation anytime and anywhere.' Traditional Buddhism defines the ideal form of Zen as Zen in conjunction with the practice of silence (refraining from speaking) and the four movements of everyday life: to go, to stay, to sit and to sleep. These two are probably referring to the same concept. In this state, one becomes completely free and is not swayed by any situation in the outside world. This is freedom in its most complete form. Ordinary human beings like us immediately lose control over ourselves when external limits are imposed. We become anxious and stressed out because we are unable to do as we wish. This is why we sometimes say "I do not even know myself," due to a lack of an inner compass. According to Sot'aesan, it is not easy to remain unswayed by external situations at first. Thus, when a situation occurs, one must study in order to remain untouched by it. While increasing the instances in which one is able to control one's own mind, Sot'aesan states that it is when one is able to remain unswayed without trying that one is truly ready.

Sot'aesan uses strong language to explain what this state of mind is like. The original term uses difficult Chinese characters, which I have translated into longhand for a Western readership to understand. When the mind becomes free, "(you) will be centered like an iron pillar and defended from the outside like a stone wall" so that neither wealth nor power can tempt the mind away. The iron pillar is a symbol of a very strong inner persona. If the outside is guarded against by a wall made of stone, how strong it must be! The expression brings to mind a state of unshakable strength that does not bow to any external threat or temptation. In any situation, the mind remains as calm as an untouched pond. Feeling that one must 'have patience' or 'let's just wait for this to pass' indicates that there is still a long way to go in terms of training. But once the highest state has been achieved, one can maintain a state of *samadhi* regardless of the situation or circumstances.

At this point, one is completely unmoved even when tempted by a huge sum of money, a position of power or an attractive man or woman. This is achieved through the Great Dharma. Although it may look difficult to do, once it is understood properly, anyone and everyone including farmers, industrial workers, and corporate and government employees can do Zen meditation in the comfort of one's home. Sot'aesan calls Zen that is practiced only while sitting or in a room 'sickly Zen.' Sickly Zen is incapable of rescuing all sentient beings. We have thus far discussed timeless Zen. I will conclude with the words of Sot'aesan himself, which require no further explanation: "When the six sense organs are free from activity, remove distracted thoughts and nurture the one mind. When the six sense organs are involved in activity, remove the wrong and nurture the right."

Training Aid 1: Keeping a Diary

Thus far, we have seen various methods of training. The descriptions of these alone are very detailed, but Sot'aesan apparently was not satisfied with these alone. Sot'aesan, who was compassionate, meticulous and most of all confident in his newly-made dharma, withheld nothing in his efforts to put together a scripture from which anyone could become enlightened. The most representative examples of this would be the dharma of keeping a diary or supplication. The purpose of the dharma of keeping a diary is to have an opportunity to self-evaluate whether or not one has devoted one's mind to a task or situation that arises in daily life. If you were mindful, a mark is made in the column 'mindfulness;' if you were not mindful, a mark is made in the column 'unmindfulness.' Also, it is encouraged to record whether that incident ended well or not. This can be seen as a call to always be awake to one's state of mind.

Wakefulness is very important in religious training. The vast majority of us live our daily lives without much thought. We do things the way they have always been done or the way that everyone else does them. Although one is technically alive, it is actually a state of slumber because you are living according to someone else's sense of self. This is the state that religious practitioners fear the most. One is still subject to error even when approaching everything in life with a strong sense of self; it would be impossible to achieve the highest state of religious consciousness by living thoughtlessly. This is why anyone who has a religion must always examine and be aware of oneself. The teachings of the Vietnamese monk Thich Naht Hanh, which have recently become popular in Korea, state the same thing. At his collective, a bell is sounded several times throughout the day. Each time the bell rings, everyone stops what they were doing and observe themselves. It is a method of checking whether one is in control of oneself or not, an opportunity for people like us who leave ourselves abandoned for most of the day to become aware.

Sot'aesan not only emphasized mindfulness and unmindfulness but also taught that it was important to keep a record of attendance at meetings or Zen training sessions. Furthermore, additional checks are done on precepts to see whether or not they are being kept.

Sot'aesan's meticulous attention to every detail goes one step further. Society was less civilized in Sot'aesan's day, and thus there were many who could not read. He directed them to mark their evaluations of mindfulness and unmindfulness with beans. The procedure is as follows. For each mindful act, a white bean was collected; for each unmindful act, a black bean was collected. These were then counted at the end. This is an act of true compassion, attempting to allow even those who are illiterate to train. Then what should be done in a society that is as busy as today's? Because the everyday routine is so hectic, there is little time to keep a diary. To suit these conditions, the Won Buddhist order has come up with the mindfulness-unmindfulness watch. The blank that would indicate the date on a normal watch is made into black and white blocks that each stand for unmindfulness and mindfulness, respectively. Pressing the switch on the watch increases the number for either black or white. At the end of the day, one can see how much of that day was spent in what way. The watch was very popular among believers when it was first created, but it is a rare sight today. Sot'aesan also recommends recording the number of hours that were spent wisely or wastefully as well as one's expenses and earnings; the latter is to always be aware of one's finances.

One may think that Sot'aesan was excessively attentive to details or that he interfered too much in the lives of his disciples. But enlightened people seem to be this way in general. Of course, this attention to detail is not the same as ordinary people being compulsive or obsessive but is an attentiveness that is meant to monitor and guide disciples' training. Sot'aesan often complained that the condition of his disciples was less than reassuring; Buddha apparently had the same issue. According to early Buddhist scripture, Buddha's nagging increased as he became older. As mentioned earlier in this book, this is very different from the image of an endlessly compassionate teacher. However, the nagging of enlightened ones is probably diametrically different from ours. Did not Mencius say that sages become angry for others while small-minded ones become angry because of themselves?

Training Aid 2: Mental Affirmation and Supplication

Perhaps it is because traditional Buddhism is a religion which aspires toward self-enlightenment that there are not many doctrines on prayer. However, in many other religions, prayer is a highly important task. The role of prayer is essential to people who seek an absolute being (deity) to the extent that it itself is seen as religion. Also, prayer provides hope and assistance to many. Well aware of this situation, Sot'aesan emphasized the importance of reaching enlightenment on one's own but did not disregard the importance of prayer when appealing to an absolute being. The object of prayer in Won Buddhism is the Dharmakaya Buddha, which allows prayer to be done almost exactly as in a theist religion. Prayers are given to Dharmakaya Buddha in hopes of being blessed by the fourfold grace, a power that we will be looking at shortly. Prayers of thanksgiving are done when something good has happened, and prayers for forgiveness are done when a wrongdoing has been committed. When having difficulties, prayer explains the situation and asks that it be changed for the better; in good times, prayer is done so that one does not become too proud.

One question that arises here is that Sot'aesan does not make a distinction between mental affirmation and prayer. The term 'mental affirmation' is thought to originate from Tonghak and is the act of informing one's innermost mind (known as Hanulnim in Tonghak) of the current situation. The two terms can be differentiated by the object of the prayer: while mental affirmation is to oneself, prayer is to an outside being. But Sot'aesan uses these terms interchangeably.

Sot'aesan taught that if continuous devotion is given to mental affirmation and supplication, the fourfold grace will be moved and one's prayers will be answered. People create a mental image before acting upon something; the more powerful this image, the stronger the power that emerges. In other words, whether or not something happens depends on how much it is hoped for. In a sense, prayer is the process of putting the individual and the universe on the same wavelength. While there is no connection with the energy of the universe in ordinary circumstances, prolonged prayer can change this, after which that immense source of energy can be easily tapped into. It is like finding the right wavelength on the radio to listen to a program.

However, Sot'aesan does not forget to emphasize that prayer also be done in a logical manner. He divides it into three categories: silent mental affirmation, practical supplication (praying to a certain being) and explanatory supplication (praying aloud before a group). Not only are the categories very specific but the fact that there is a type of prayer for each situation is a wonderful concept. If there is a being to whom to direct the prayer, all three types can be used, but if not it is possible to forego practical supplication. As we have seen, even the instructions for prayer are impeccably precise.

Training Aid 3: Everywhere a Buddha Image, Every Act a Buddha Offering

Let us now look at the last section on training: the dharma of Buddha offering. Sot'aesan had many objections to how offering was done in traditional Buddhism. Because we discussed this in detail in a previous chapter, it will be covered only briefly here. Buddhists always prayed before a Buddha statue for any situation, which Sot'aesan believed was foolish. Instead, what is to be asked of heaven should be asked of heaven, and the same applies for parents, friends and the law. In other words, prayer should be directed to each of the four graces. However, there is no place in the universe that does not have a Buddha statue. This is because everything in the universe is derived from Buddhadharma, who changed his own form to become all objects. This is why everywhere is a Buddha image. This may be an alien concept to Western readers but it is a common facet of many Eastern religions. This has been interpreted in folk religions to be animism, or the belief that all things are imbued with a spirit. Korean shamanism also adheres to the belief that "all things in the world are alive," also known as pantheism in religious studies. Everywhere a Buddha image, although slightly different in nuance, can be seen as a similar concept to that of pantheism or animism as it is defined by Buddhism.

However, Sot'aesan did not simply regard this as a nice theory but used every opportunity to put it into practice. One day, a tour group came to visit Won Buddhist headquarters. Seeing that there was no Buddha statue in the temple, the group asked where it was kept. Sot'aesan responded without missing a beat that "our Buddha is not in right now, but will return soon." "What? Outside?" The visitors were naturally confused by the situation. Moments later, Sot'aesan's disciples returned with farm tools over their shoulders. Sot'aesan pointed them out, saying "these people are our Buddhas." The scripture states that the visitors then became even more confused. Of course, this story represents the Buddhist doctrine that all sentient beings are Buddha. However, traditional Buddhism tends to limit the definition of Buddha only to the statue inside the temple; it does not award the same term to ordinary people in the way that was done in the story. On the other hand, Sot'aesan applied this doctrine directly to everyday life. The ultimate application of it is of course found in the Il-Won-Sang image in the temple.

Because all things are Buddha, everything that one does becomes an offering to Buddha. Thus, 'every act a Buddha offering.' We have already seen this concept in our discussion of giving offerings to Buddha, which is a familiar doctrine in not only Korean religions but Eastern religion as a whole. Sot'aesan added to this the dimension of time. In the past it was believed that offerings could be given at any time, but Sot'aesan argued that there is a certain timeframe to be kept for each situation. There are things for which offerings should be given for several lifetimes—because Sot'aesan believed in the literal existence of reincarnation, it was entirely possible to be devoted throughout lifetimes—and others that should only take up several days; each situation had to be matched. This is the giving of true Buddha offerings, also a very pragmatic solution.

We have now finished going through training methods in Won Buddhism. Before I conclude, I would like to introduce something that is always chanted by Won Buddhists. It is called 'The Essential Dharmas of Daily Practice.' Won Buddhists recite these verses while training throughout the day. I have quoted the scripture verbatim in order to convey the feel of the original text.

• The Essential Dharmas of Daily Practice •

1. The mind ground is originally free from disturbance, but disturbances arise in response to sensory conditions; let us give rise to the absorption of the self-nature by letting go of those disturbances.
2. The mind ground is originally free from delusion, but delusions arise in response to sensory conditions; let us give rise to the wisdom of the self-nature by letting go of those delusions.
3. The mind ground is originally free from wrong-doing, but wrong-doings arise in response to the sensory conditions; let us give rise to the precepts of the self-nature by letting go of those wrong-doings.
4. Let use remove unbelief, greed, laziness, and foolishness by means of belief, zeal, questioning, and dedication.
5. Let us turn a life of resentment into a life of gratitude.
6. Let us turn a life of despondency into a life of self-reliance.

7. Let us turn a reluctance to learn into a readiness to learn well.
8. Let us turn a reluctance to teach into a readiness to teach well.
9. Let us turn a lack of public spirit into an eagerness for the public's welfare.

About Truth

If the trainee continues to practice in the ways that we have just discussed, his or her eyes will eventually become opened to truth, the way that humans and the universe can communicate. The trainee comes face to face with what is called 'ultimate reality' in religious studies. Ultimate reality is basically 'really real reality' or the origin of all things. All things in the world constantly change and are part of the inevitable cycle of birth and death, but there is something behind this that triggers all of the change. Of course, there are schools that deny the existence of any such thing, but most religions do define this reality and it comes in many forms. For example, there is Dharmakaya Buddha, Brahman, God, the Way, Nothingness and so on.

Sot'aesan decided to call it *Il-Won-Sang*. The Chinese character for 'won' literally means 'circle,' the symbol for perfection. A circle has no beginning or end and always returns to the same place; although it can technically be seen as made up of many straight lines, it is essentially round. Therefore, all shapes can fit inside it—not only can the hexagon, another symbol for perfection, fit exactly inside but other shapes like a square or triangle can all fit as well. It encompasses all shapes, which is why many religions use the circle to symbolize truth. The best representation of this is the Buddhist *mandala*. A *mandala* is a drawing of the fundamental state of the enlightened mind. It is laid out in perfectly symmetrical designs, and the circle is the shape that is most often used. Analytical psychologist Carl G. Jung became interested in the Buddhist *mandala* after seeing the pictures that his patients drew of their dreams. The pictures often contain very simple shapes, most of which are circles (i. e., a snake that has eaten its tail). This was interpreted to be patients intentionally drawing the most perfect shape in order to idealize what their innermost egos look like and attempt to heal themselves by drawing them. In this way, regardless of culture or religion, the circle is the shape that best symbolizes perfection. Whether or not Sot'aesan knew all of this, it was very wise of him to decide on the circle as the symbol of his new religion.

What is the Il-Won-Sang?

Sot'aesan, in the spirit of Eastern philosophy, describes fundamental reality as 'substance' and 'function.' Substance indicates origin or root, and function is the appearance of substance. There is only one section of explanation on the *Il-Won-Sang*, but it definitely does cover both substance and function. Let us see how its fundamental appearance is described:

> The original source of all things in the universe
> The mind-seal of all the Buddhas and sages
> The original nature of all sentient beings
> The realm where there is no discrimination regarding great and small, being and nonbeing
> The realm where wholesome and unwholesome karmic retribution has ceased

> The realm where languages, names, and characteristics are utterly void

The above description seems to include all the terms traditionally used in the East to explain ultimate reality. There is no need for a great deal of explanation here, because it is a level that exceeds human understanding. Because human beings are unable to understand anything without using language, this state that transcends all language is literally beyond understanding. Hinduism has called Brahman, who has no qualities or properties, Nirguna Brahman. Because this Brahman has no properties, human beings are unable to understand it. Then are humans doomed to never understand Brahman? This is not the case. Below Nirguna Brahman there is another Brahman called Saguna Brahman, one that does have properties and thus is able to be understood. Of course, the latter is one level beneath ultimate reality, but otherwise we would never be able to envision an absolute being like Brahman. To attempt an example, it is like the difference between the Unnamable and the Namable essences, terms that appear in the first chapter of Lao Zi's *Tao Te Ching* (*Dao De Jing*). Then how does Sot'aesan explain the dimension of *Il-Won-Sang* that we are capable of understanding?

This section is actually not very long, but it is where the difference becomes apparent. According to one's spiritual state, there are different levels as well as good and bad *karma*. It can be expressed by language and it is as if the entire universe is in the palm of one's hand, clear as a marble. In this state, everything in the world can alternate between voidness and being; all of this occurs freely. This is where Sot'aesan's explanation ends. I have translated his words into modern language, which has probably lost much of the 'feel' of the original text, so that readers who are unfamiliar with Buddhist terminology and references can understand what was meant. But for the sake of understanding this 'feel,' I will introduce the most important text in Won Buddhism. It is the *Il-Won-Sang* Vow.

The *Il-Won-Sang* Vow

Il-Won is the realm of Samadhi beyond all words and speech, the gateway of birth and death that transcends being and non-being, the original source of heaven and earth, parents, fellow beings, and laws, and the nature of all Buddhas, enlightened masters, ordinary humans, and sentient beings. It can form both the permanent and the impermanent: viewed as the permanent, it has unfolded into an infinite world that is ever abiding and unextinguished, just as it is and spontaneous; viewed as the impermanent, it has unfolded into an infinite world, now as progression, now as regression, here as grace arising from harm, there as harm arising from grace, by effecting transformations through the formation, subsistence, decay, and extinction of the universe, the birth, old age, sickness, and death of all things, and the six destinies in accordance with the mental and physical functions of the four types of birth. Therefore, modeling ourselves wholeheartedly on this *Il-Won-Sang*, the Dharmakaya Buddha, and practicing with utmost devotion to keep our mind and body perfectly, to know human affairs and universal principles perfectly, and to use our mind and body perfectly, we deluded beings make this vow so that, by progressing rather than regressing and receiving grace rather than harm, we may attain the awesome power of *Il-Won* and be unified with the essential nature of *Il-Won*.

This vow in Won Buddhism has the weight of the *Prajna Sutra* in traditional Buddhism. Sot'aesan included all the truth that he had become awakened to into this short statement. Just as monks recite the *Prajna Sutra* each time they worship before the Buddha, Won Buddhist ministers recite this vow at each service. Now that we have pretty much exhausted the *Il-Won-Sang*, let us know look at Sot'aesan's summary of the principles of *Il-Won*. It was mentioned earlier, and is called the Transmission Verse for short.

> Being into nonbeing and nonbeing into being,
> Turning and turning—in the ultimate,
> Being and nonbeing are both void,
> Yet this void is also complete.

Because any interpretation of this would be a clumsy one, I will leave it up to the reader. But I would imagine that it roughly means "because being and nonbeing are relative concepts, they complement each other in a constantly repeating cycle; everything is empty without features, but if you look closely it is actually full." What we will now turn our attention to is the content of the *Il-Won*, the aspect that Sot'aesan emphasized the most. According to him, the actual 'meat and bones' of *Il-Won* is the Fourfold Grace, which I have referred to countless times throughout this book. I call the grace defined by Sot'aesan 'Great Grace' to differentiate it from the grace that we normally envision, because it is the most fundamental force in the universe. Let us look at each of them closely.

The Fourfold Grace

According to Sot'aesan, everything in the universe or nature is a transformation of Dharmakaya Buddha; these things are brought into being in human beings' relationships with them as distributors of grace. As we have now seen so many times, these four graces are: Grace of Heaven and Earth, Grace of Parents, Grace of Fellow Beings and Grace of Laws. They can be connected together in the following way. Because I came into being within the boundaries of nature or this universe, nature is an object of boundless gratitude. We cannot exist without very specific conditions of nature. However, although I was born into the world in nature, I would not be here without my parents. In addition, our parents have even more grace because they raised us from infancy. The position of parents in this hierarchy of grace is self-explanatory. But one does not live out one's life in the world alone. It is impossible to survive without a community. One cannot eat without the farmer who grows the food or be clothed without the tailor who makes the clothes. This is the grace of fellow beings. The coexistence of many people in the same space inevitably brings about clashes and conflict. There needs to be laws and regulations to control this conflict. This is the grace of laws. With that, the Fourfold Grace is made complete as a religious doctrine. However, there are a few questions that come to mind.

Firstly, the Fourfold Grace takes up the most space on Sot'aesan's doctrinal chart and is the longest section of the parts that explain doctrine. The biggest question arises here: why does the concept of grace take up such a large percentage of Won Buddhist doctrine? Traditional Buddhism has a lot of explanation that deals with how to become enlightened, but it does not go into much detail about things like grace. But Sot'aesan makes grace the basic doctrine of the universe. Furthermore, Grace of Fellow Beings and the Grace of Laws—the latter in particular—are obscure and artificial-looking concepts that have virtually no place in Buddhism. In *Chŏngjŏn*, the section that deals with the Fourfold Grace is much longer than that on *Il-Won-Sang*, the embodiment of truth. In this case, should the Fourfold Grace not have been discussed in greater detail in *Taejonggyŏng*? However, this does not seem to be the case even with a cursory reading of *Taejonggyŏng*. If *Taejonggyŏng* truly believed that the Fourfold Grace was a priority, it should have been given more room.

To explain the Grace of Heaven and Earth, Sot'aesan borrows from Lao Zi's interpretation of morals. The way of heaven and earth is the spontaneous method in which the "great mechanism of the universe (a sort of framework)" works; the manifestation of the Way is the virtue of the universe. The Way of the universe is composed of various qualities such as exceeding radiance, steadfastness, justness, natural orderliness, eternal and imperishable, among many others. In particular, not only the earth and sky but also the sun and moon, wind, clouds, rain and dew allow human beings to survive; this is grace. In a modern interpretation, the grace of the atmosphere should be included in the above list. Life is able to exist on earth because the atmosphere blocks ultraviolet rays. With the birth of modern natural science, people have come to realize that the atmosphere is the most basic element necessary for survival; even if there is oxygen and water, life would not be possible without the atmosphere to block out the sun's rays.

Of course, the universe that Sot'aesan is referring to is a concept that transcends all of these natural elements and conscious understanding in general. This is because heaven and earth administer either fortune or disaster based on whether or not we follow the way of the universe. Sot'aesan advises us to respect the way of the universe; among his explanations is an interesting point that discourages being obsessed with fortune. One could go about this in the following way: find something negative in a good situation, and find something positive in a bad situation. In another section Sot'aesan rephrases this same concept. One should always exercise caution, but one should try especially hard to prepare for disaster amidst prosperity and find something good amidst disaster. One has to be more careful in good situations than bad ones because this is the more difficult thing to do. It is easy to become overly confident during good times; in this case, one ends up unwittingly falling into difficulty. Sot'aesan encourages us to always follow the way of the universe so that we do not fall victim to this course of events. While these explanations are understandable, they are highly theoretical and thus seem distant from our current lives. I also want to ask Sot'aesan how he knows the workings of the universe. This interpretation of the universe in purely ethical terms seems to be influenced by Confucianism. The next grace is the Grace of Parents, which is a central tenet of Confucianism. It would have been impossible to discuss grace in Chosŏn, a nation built on Confucianism, without including that of one's parents.

Let us move directly on to the Grace of Fellow Beings. I have explained this is as the grace of one's community, but its definition is actually much broader in scope. Sot'aesan interprets 'fellow beings' to include not only people but also animals, trees and even grass. Human beings can live only by being tightly interconnected with all sorts of living things. This grace is also fairly self-explanatory. Sot'aesan states that one must always act fairly to people of all occupations and thus allow both parties to be profitable—this would be called a win-win situation in today's terms. Interestingly, animals are not to be butchered and trees and plants are not to be cut down without due cause.

In explaining the Grace of Laws, Sot'aesan quotes the concept of "self-cultivation for individuals, domestic affairs for families, social order for societies, national order for nations and global order for the world" which appears in the Confucian text *The Great Learning* and argues that there needs to be laws at each level. If not, all indications of peace and order in the world may vanish. All of this is completely understandable. However, there is one aspect of this grace that remains confusing. For the previous three Graces of Heaven and Earth, Parents and Fellow Beings, these are appropriately designated as graces because these three are the suppliers of grace and we are the receiving agents. But for the Grace of Laws, laws work only through mutual agreement to abide by them: mutual agreement, by definition, is not grace. Furthermore, we are obligated to follow laws and regulations by default, which I also wonder if it can be considered grace.

We have now seen all aspects of what Sot'aesan believed to be fundamental truth. Then, what is someone who has become enlightened to all of this supposed to do about it? Sot'aesan, unlike most Buddhist philosophers, was highly interested in the construction of a just society. Buddhists, who are too focused on self-enlightenment, tend to not care about the outside world. But it is all too common knowledge that an individual cannot exist alone without society. If society is ill, the individual cannot remain healthy no matter how hard he or she may try. In this sense, Sot'aesan's interest in societal health is perfectly natural. Let us now uncover what he wanted to do about it.

How to create a just society—Serving the Community

When we think of religious figures, the image that usually comes to mind is a person who only discusses lofty subjects. But most of those that they teach are 'common folk,' and so much of what they teach is about things in everyday life. For example, Buddha once gave a dharma talk about the need for "husbands to buy jewels for their wives," an entirely commonplace subject. Thus, it is actually not strange at all for Sot'aesan to have been interested in social issues in addition to enlightenment. Moreover, Korea at the time was a Japanese colony, a situation in which societal ills would have been easily noticeable for Sot'aesan.

As I have already mentioned in the chapter on Sot'aesan's life, the first sermon that he gave after becoming enlightened was how the strong and the weak should live together in society. In particular, he criticized the unjustness of the strong abusing the weak and made several analogies of this. The most famous analogy is that of a tadpole in a dry pond. The story itself is very simple. A dried up pond became filled up with water after the monsoon season and it soon attracted many frogs. This resulted in the sudden increase of tadpoles. But as the sun came back out, the water level visibly reduced. Sot'aesan felt pity for the tadpoles, who had no idea that their life spans were becoming shorter by the second. He equated this fate with that of people who only know how to spend money or those who are so confident in their abilities that they abuse others. This analogy seems to have been directed at the Japanese colonial authorities.

The fact that Sot'aesan's first sermon was about how the strong and the weak can coexist indicates that he was very much interested in creating an ideal society. On top of this, science was developing rapidly and pushing human civilization into a period of great change and turmoil. It was the beginning of the reign of material civilization. With all this in mind, Sot'aesan condensed his teaching into the slogan "With this great opening of matter, let there be a great opening of spirit." Humanity was thus at the brink of a seemingly bright future within the broad sweep of history, but Korea was in a precarious situation as a Japanese colony after the collapse of the feudalistic Chosŏn dynasty. Sot'aesan summarized these points into his illustration of a society that was ill and in critical condition.

An Ill Society and its Treatment

According to Sot'aesan, an ill society displays the following symptoms. First of all, people do not realize their own faults and only blame others. Also, people become overly dependent on the bounty of others, and those who are supposed to learn do not try to learn and teachers do not try to teach. 'Public spirit' is the giving of what is beneficial and convenient to others and keeping what is inconvenient for oneself; a society that does not have many people who are public spirited is an ill society. By this standard, our own society is indeed very ill.

Sot'aesan provides more specific advice on this illness. From his perspective, society at the time was too caught up in material possessions; if this desire was not overcome in the near future, the illness would become too deep for recovery. His diagnosis of society was the following. First and foremost, money is illness. It is an illness that causes one to abandon any sense of loyalty or 'face' because you would be too busy spending money on fulfilling desires. If this trend continues, society loses its ethical standard and mutual affection between individuals becomes thin. Because all of this can easily be seen today, I will move onto the next point in Sot'aesan's diagnosis.

The second illness is the illness of resentment. As the wording suggests, it is an illness in which people are always blaming one another. I forget about the grace shown to me by others, but I never forget the grace that I may have provided to someone else. Because everyone is too busy shifting blame, there is always a continuous stream of disputes small and large. We saw just earlier that this is still valid today. As with the other illnesses, this one is closely related to personal maturity and interpersonal skills. The more mature the personality, less blame is directed toward others and most of it is placed on oneself. One is too busy trying to remove the plank in one's own eye to see the tic in someone else's eye. Small children find the source of most of their problems outside themselves. Anything that goes wrong is always because of something in the outside world, not the self.

According to Sot'aesan, the difference between an ascetic and an ordinary person on resentment and gratitude is as the following. An ordinary person, even if a benefactor has been good to him ten times, will turn all of it into resentment if the benefactor makes one mistake. On the other hand, an ascetic will be thankful if a person who has wronged ten times does well even once. Thus, ordinary people are always unhappy because they are so busy finding bad things amidst grace, and ascetics are always happy because they always manage to find grace amidst even the worst situation. Also, ordinary people only care about their own business, thinking that they are intelligent. But most of this ends in failure. On the other hand, a bodhisattva seems foolish because he or she is always doing something on behalf of someone else, but eventually receives his reward. This comparison, like the previous one, would also be right at home in today's world. People with mature personalities never blame their surroundings or others no matter how difficult the situation may be, because they know that this does not solve anything. But even today, there is no corner of society in which the shout of resentment cannot be heard. This is because society as a whole is not yet mature. It seems that our society will need a lot more time before this becomes possible.

The third illness is the illness of dependency. It is the desire to make a profit by depending on someone else. Sot'aesan pointed out that this illness is especially prevalent among Koreans, because Korea spent hundreds of years indulging *yangban* at the expense of abandoning military statecraft. This was probably in reference to the entire Chosŏn dynasty. The same criticism was made by several intellectuals toward the end of the dynasty. Chŏng Yakyong, one of the most liberal intellectuals of his day, wrote that people enjoy depending on others to the point that if one person works, there are ten others who parasitically attach themselves to him. The fact that Sot'aesan points out the same problem indicates that this truly must have been a serious issue.

The illnesses continue. The fourth one is the illness of not learning. The acts of learning and teaching were very important to Sot'aesan. It is said that 90 percent of our personality is formed by what we learn as opposed to being biologically inherited. Therefore, no matter who the other person is, if there is something to be learned from that person one must be ready to take this in. But most people lose these types of opportunities because of pride. The next illness is closely related to this one. The fifth illness is the illness of not knowing how to teach. No matter how much knowledge a person may have, it is useless if he or she is unwilling to share it with others. There are people in the world who, out of excessive confidence in his or her intellect, refuse to mingle with the less educated; this is also a serious illness. These two (fourth and fifth) illnesses have aspects that are understandable and others that are not. While it is understandable that Koreans at the time were lazy and did not invest effort in teaching and learning, it is difficult to imagine that the education-oriented culture of Confucianism had absolutely no effect at all. In any case, these two illnesses do not seem to be a problem today. In fact, there are too many college entrance 'cram schools' that study too much useless information, but this is a topic for an entirely different book.

The last illness is the illness of a lack of public spirit. This illness is also fully understandable. Sot'aesan believed Korea had a several thousand year-old tradition of selfishness that had only solidified over the passing millennia. This was why there was a constant shortage of people willing to serve others, and even those who began community service with a heart of sacrifice quit in the middle for want of personal gain. Koreans, both then and now, not only have trouble differentiating the public and private domains but also have little understanding of a public-oriented mind. Today's lack of a philanthropic culture is probably a result of this long-standing tendency. There are two reasons behind this state of affairs. Firstly, Korean society is still immature, therefore meaning that the average Korean has not yet reached a mature state of mind. An individual is fully matured when he or she prioritizes the larger community before oneself. The most mature type of person goes beyond humanity and equates his or her fate with that of all living things and always tries to work for the good of the whole. In short, it is a transcending of oneself. On the other hand, an immature person acts in exactly the opposite direction. There are many indications that Koreans in general are still at the immature stage.

Degree of maturity is also influenced by a sociocultural factor. Koreans too frequently draw dividing lines between 'us' and 'them.' Anyone who is not in my group is relegated to 'them.' Thus, there is no need to pay attention to other people. To tell such Koreans to think of one comprehensive group—society—is a difficult task at best. This is why there is no public spirit or conscience. While things have begun to improve in recent years, this is limited to a minority and is not prevalent among Korean society as a whole. If there are still so many societal ills left today, what must things have been like back then? Sot'aesan expresses this same concern in an address before the Buddhist Dharma Society in 1924: "We who were in a collective stupor, in a drunken lapse, were prevented from receiving a proper education due to the order of scholar-farmer-industrialist-merchant[2]... did not receive the benefits of foreign civilizations, did not have logic or reason, had no work to do and thus were idle..." Sot'aesan's self-critique reflects the general sentiment of people living in the colonial period. However, he was not hung up on self-blame and inferiority complexes. As we will see in more detail later, he declared that Korea would continue to develop into one of the world's strongest nations. Just as a fish turns into a dragon.

---

2 Sot'aesan is referring to the social hierarchy of Chosŏn, listed in decreasing order of respectability. The Confucian standard for class was degree of education in the Chinese classics. Only those who had the financial means to be able to spend years studying (as well as the right family pedigree) could become government officials, the highest class.

The Cure for an Ill Society

We have just seen Sot'aesan's diagnosis of the diseased society that was Korea. A good doctor not only makes a proper diagnosis but also offers an appropriate remedy. Sot'aesan called his remedy 'the four essentials.' It must have been an important concept to him, as we can see it listed in *Chŏngjŏn* right after the Fourfold Grace. In terms of the whole, the four essentials are near the front of the book. This shows how important this concept was to Sot'aesan. The four essentials are: developing self power, the wise one first, educating others' children and venerating the public-spirited. With these, Sot'aesan believed that a civilized egalitarian society could be built.

The first article, developing self power, means exactly what the wording suggests: achieving independence through the cultivation of one's own abilities. As we discussed earlier, people in the past were overly dependent on the labor of others for their day-to-day survival. Of the various forms of dependence, the phenomenon that Sot'aesan criticized the most was society's disempowerment of women. In his eyes, women of the past were bundles of dependence. They were never free to control their own destinies: before marriage, a woman was dependent on her father; after marriage, she was dependent on her husband; and after her husband's death, she was dependent on her son. Women were not allowed to be educated, have friends or have a share of the family inheritance. Sot'aesan's critique of women's social conditions is today common knowledge that anyone would agree with. The interesting fact here is that Sot'aesan was deeply concerned about the plight of women. Not only were there always many female disciples, but among all the founders of new religions in Korea,

Sot'aesan was the one who awarded women the most leadership positions. We will look at Sot'aesan and Won Buddhism's perspective on women in a later section.

Then how is this situation to be fixed? First of all, a person who has the ability to fend for himself or herself but tries to depend on someone else should be discouraged from doing so. This can damage the individual's ego. The next article is a highly practical piece of advice. Parents are directed to not only divide the inheritance equally among all sons instead of only to the eldest son, but also to include daughters as well. However, Sot'aesan allowed that the inheritance can be withheld from a son or daughter if there was just cause to believe that he or she was incapable of managing it. Sot'aesan's practical nature is evident all the more considering that the very idea of equal division of the family inheritance for all of the children was a revolutionary one. It is only in the early 1990s that this concept was formally made into law, showing just how far ahead Sot'aesan was of Korean society. Before his emergence, inheritance in the Chosŏn dynasty was an exclusive right of the eldest son, the rationale for which was that the eldest son required extra financial support in order to perform ancestral rites. Daughters were not given anything because they were considered part of their husband's family and thus did not require further investment by their natal families. This harsh policy—although it was at least partly legitimate at the time—was administered until recently; Sot'aesan had already rejected it during the colonial period. The issue of the inheritance and ancestral rites is an important key to understanding the Chosŏn dynasty.

Sot'aesan did more to ease the plight of women. Women were not only to receive the same education as men but also have a job outside the home. This state of equality is to continue for the woman's entire life. Thus, husband and wife were to each have independent financial means even after marriage. This is a highly important point. Koreans until recently believed that it was normal for a woman to depend entirely on her husband financially. A husband would angrily refuse and think that his wife was underestimating him if she expressed the desire to earn money. Of course the opposite of this is becoming more customary these days, but to suggest that women could work outside the home during the colonial period was nothing short of revolutionary. In fact, it was borderline heresy. The concept of equality of the sexes is nothing new today, but it needs to be considered within the social context of colonial Korea. Sot'aesan made all of his principles in utmost peace of mind, but among these were many radical concepts. Did Buddha not say that this is like "a typhoon rushing onto a calm sea?"

Let us move onto the next article: the wise one first. This should be understood as a call for learning to be embedded into everyday life and for educated people to take a leading role in society. One important condition of learning was that it should not be influenced by the unequal social order of the day. I have just discussed several things that Sot'aesan found wrong or lacking in Korean society at the time. He always said that anyone, regardless of race, gender, age, legitimate birth (offspring of first/primary wife or concubine) or class who had any redeeming qualities should be learned from. I mentioned the importance of learning in the section describing an ill society. This was most likely a criticism of the weakness of Korean society.

The next article—educating others' children—is an unusual one. It means that the new generation should always be thoroughly educated. Because of the weak social infrastructure, there were many people who had never received an education. This was especially true of those in the lower classes and women. However, education is a critical component in the formation of a developed society; thus, as many people as possible should be given the benefit of formal education. This is why Sot'aesan insisted that all children, whether one's own or not, should be sent to school. He also strongly encouraged his flock to make monetary donations to schools, meaning that the goal should be the education of all children rather than only one's own. Indeed, one of the reasons behind Korea's rapid development is the power of public education.

However, overemphasis on education creates its own abuses. In other words, it opens up the era of unlimited competition in which only one's own child is important. In terms of their children, Korean mothers expect only one thing: to enter a good university. If my child can go to a good university, neither bribing teachers nor private tutoring is too much money to spare. Contrary to Sot'aesan's wishes, most Koreans mothers are reluctant to invest their money in public schools. They do not care that the quality of education in public institutions, i.e. schools, is getting progressively worse due to lack of funding. There is no need to care, because the child can be privately tutored or attend a cram school. This practice has been termed the 'my child first' syndrome (the person that Korean mothers fear the most is the mother next door). Korean education today is in dire straits because of 'my child first' syndrome. I cannot help but wonder whether Sot'aesan actually foresaw this, having insisted on allowing all children a fair chance at education from the colonial period. It seems that enlightened people are able to see through things clearly regardless of time and space.

The last article is venerating the public-spirited. Its principle is easy enough to understand. If society is to run smoothly, there need to be many dedicated workers who devote themselves to the public good. Sot'aesan firmly believed that in the future there would be many public-spirited people, because the society of the future would treat them with respect. Among the various societal wrongs that Sot'aesan points out, the tendency of most people to discriminate against those outside their own circle is an interesting one. This criticism is probably aimed at societal norms of that period, which mostly consisted of dividing people by family name and place of origin. Because of heavy Confucian influence, people made clear divisions between their own family and other families. This developed further over time to create "Weism," one of the most serious handicaps of Korean society today. It is a viciously exclusive practice that only favors my own family, my hometown and my school. Weism worms its way into the public sphere as well, preventing fair evaluation based on ability and only giving preference to people directly connected to oneself. Thus, conditions are such that truly public-spirited workers are rare, because for Koreans there only exists the small community that they are directly involved in. In this case, any sense of a large unifying community is virtually nonexistent. Sot'aesan seems to have foreseen this tendency as well. He predicted that many enlightened people would emerge, thus allowing public-minded people to be properly recognized for their efforts. I do not think this has yet come true in Korean society.

Features of an Ideal Society 1: No Discrimination based on gender

In Sot'aesan's remedy for an ill society, the need to overcome discrimination against women is mentioned time and time again. Like Chŭngsan, Sot'aesan was interested in the problems faced by women and came to the obvious conclusion that something needed to be done. As an ardent supporter of universalism, there is little chance that he remains silent on discrimination against women. Sot'aesan was constantly surrounded by female disciples. I suspect that his masculine aura must have been extremely attractive to the women who knew him. Several of them are still alive today, and all of them had a great deal of respect and love for Sot'aesan. This can only have been true because they willingly devoted their lives to following him and his laws.

Sot'aesan not only spoke of gender equality but wasted no time in putting this into action. The leaders of Chŭngsangyo (Chŭngsan religion) and Chŏndogyo (Tonghak) both supported equality between the sexes, but this does not seem to have been actually applied in either case. One easy yardstick for gender equality is the number of women in positions of influence within the religion; neither of the above two religions had many women in positions of power. However, Won Buddhism not only allowed women to enter the priesthood but placed them in influential positions. The fact that women are allowed to have leadership positions within the religion at all is very rare; Buddhism seems to be the only other case of this. It is still forbidden in the Catholic Church and only condoned in isolated cases in the Protestant Church.

But one look at the group that led the religion in its early days shows that women occupied many of the positions and played a significant role. Furthermore, the Supreme Dharma Council—the highest decision-making body of Won Buddhism—was composed of men and women in equal numbers from the very beginning. Imagine that half of the cardinals below the Pope in the Vatican are women; how strange this seems! In 2003, for the first time a woman was appointed as Director-General of Administration in Won Buddhism. The Director-General of Administration is roughly equivalent to the Director of General Affairs in Buddhism, the highest administrative position. Imagine a female monk as the Director of General Affairs in the Chogye order, the largest order of Korean Buddhism. When a female monk was appointed as Director of Culture a few years ago, the Chogye order made a huge deal out of it, calling it a revolutionary move. But it is something that had already been done in Won Buddhism decades earlier. Now we may be able to see a woman in the highest position in Won Buddhism, the Prime Dharma Master (however, keep in mind that there were no women among Sot'aesan's first nine disciples).

Because women have so much influence within the religion, 90 percent of Won Buddhist temples in Seoul are headed by female ministers. Of course, most of their subordinate ministers are men. This seems so normal in Won Buddhism, but imagining the same situation in the Catholic Church seems bizarre. Imagine the head priest of a church being a woman, with young male priests serving her! This shows just how advanced Won Buddhism was in its stance on women. Of course, women may feel that there is still a long way to go for true equality. As an example, male ministers are permitted to marry while female ministers are not, which brings up the question of whether or not this is discriminatory against women. This is certainly a legitimate point. The order would probably respond that if female ministers are permitted to marry, they would be too busy taking care of their children and families to devote time to religious work. But this argument seems flawed. The natural course of action would be to create more day care centers so that female ministers can still do full-time religious work; assuming that women are tied to the home is a very different view from that of Sot'aesan. Furthermore, there were various married women in the early days of Won Buddhism who had successful careers as ministers.

Late Prime Dharma Master Chŏngsan seems to have had a very radical view on the matter of women serving in the temple. While this is not conclusive evidence because it is based on oral records, it is entirely possible that Chŏngsan did hold the following view. Because a world of hedonism and pleasure was fast approaching, unmarried male and female ministers would be a rare sight. Therefore, although it is forbidden for female ministers to marry, there would be no reason in the future to prevent them from marrying. Chŏngsan assumed that it was his duty to continue his teacher's tradition of progressive doctrine even on women. It is a statement that shows the full maturity of an enlightened leader. But Won Buddhism even today can be said to have obliterated many discriminatory measures against women. It is to the extent that male ministers often remark "the women in our order are so strong that we have a hard time making ourselves heard."

Sot'aesan was not referring only to ministers when discussing gender equality. As we have seen previously, he was also very much interested in married lay believers. The most interesting point is the order for both husband and wife to each have financial means of support. In most cases, the power balance in a married couple is determined by who the breadwinner is. Women in the past did not earn money and thus had no power to speak their minds to their husbands. Also, even if women were treated unfairly and wanted to leave, it was impossible because they had no way of providing for themselves. Well aware of all this, Sot'aesan encouraged women to have jobs and be financially independent. Because most people with the exception of a tiny minority are governed by their material needs, this is a very important aspect of life. If women were to make money outside the home, their husbands would have to treat them much more carefully. Sot'aesan predicted that in the future, the sign on the door of each home would display the names of both husband and wife; I wonder if this was not an outright rejection of the patriarchal system that only saw a man as the head of a household. The following fact is also unconfirmed, but Sot'aesan also said that couples would eventually live in separate houses. This was probably aimed at the weakest aspect of any married relationship: the existence of independent selves within a single entity. In all honesty, it is not always a good thing for a couple to constantly be in the same space. Being together all the time causes a great deal of unforeseen conflict. As a wise man once said, the most ideal relationship is the weekend couple.

Features of an Ideal Society 2: The Birth of 'Real' Buddhism

Sot'aesan's idea of an ideal society included a reformation of Buddhism, because for him, Buddhism was the religion of truth. He believed that the best religion in the world had hit an all-time low. In response, Sot'aesan wrote *A Treaty on the Reformation of Korean Buddhism* (1936), which was mentioned earlier in this book. But because he was not a regular monk in the Buddhist tradition, no one paid attention to what he had to say. This is not the right attitude to have; it is the content of the criticism rather than the person who makes the criticism that should be given the spotlight. Let us now take a look at his views.

First of all, he problematized the way that traditional Buddhism was designed only to suit the purposes of the priesthood. It is difficult for ordinary people to visit temples because they are often located deep inside mountains. People who have jobs are unable to go whenever they wish. Moreover, Buddhist scriptures are written in Chinese characters, many of which are so obscure that even educated people have difficulty reading them. Becoming a monk is difficult as well; it requires one to deny everything in the secular world, have no other job and live only on donations from temple visitors. This is not all. Buddhist monks are traditionally not permitted to marry; Sot'aesan saw that this was nearly impossible for most people to adhere to. If you look into ceremonial procedures of traditional Buddhism, there is indeed a diverse range of ceremonies but nothing that is actually necessary in everyday life like weddings and funerals.

Then what is the solution? It would be to make everything the opposite of what it currently is. One of the most revolutionary measures that Sot'aesan proposed was to have no distinction between married and celibate believers. Although now there are terms like 'minister' for those in the priesthood, lay believers were originally called 'regular believers' and those who had entered the priesthood were called 'ordained believers.' In other words, married and unmarried Won Buddhists were considered equals in faith. Those who wished to focus on doctrinal study and proselytizing could become part of the clergy, and those who had other forms of livelihood could live and practice as regular believers. This type of revolution is not new; the reforms that were carried out two thousand years ago in Mahayana Buddhism reflect the same sentiment. Once monks tried to keep their access to privileges exclusive to the priesthood, regular believers instated regulatory measures. Because it is human nature to want to be placed on a pedestal, monks wish to be honored and respected by lay believers and bask in the powers of the office. It is not easy to overcome such temptations; Won Buddhism also seems to have come to a fork in the road in terms of this. The standard conclusion is that the voice of regular believers is growing increasingly less influential. It remains to be seen what new reforms will be put in place.

Won Buddhism strives to achieve a form of Buddhism that is conducive to normal everyday life. Therefore, training is not limited to only temples or hideouts deep in the mountains. Places for training should be located wherever believers are regardless of the type of location, whether it is the city or the mountains. This is why most Won Buddhist temples today are in cities. Actually, this is nothing new. During the Shilla and Koryŏ dynasties (the two dynasties before Chosŏn), most large temples were located in the cities. Hwangryong Temple, built in the sixth century and used exclusively by the royal family, was inside Kyŏngju—although it had nothing to do with ordinary believers—and Songak (present-day Kaesŏng, a city in North Korea) was filled with temples. As most Koreans know, temples were only chased out into the mountains in the Chosŏn dynasty because of persecution of Buddhism. Sot'aesan wanted to correct this state of affairs. Not only was the location of temples problematic, but scriptures in traditional Buddhism were (and are still) too esoteric, long and complicated. Sot'aesan, fully aware of these limitations, intentionally composed Won Buddhist scripture of the bare essentials and made it very easy to read. The result of these efforts is *Chŏngjŏn*. In addition, *Taejonggyŏng*, a collection of Sot'aesan's words, is written in vernacular colloquial Korean; this makes it not only easy to read but enjoyable to read as well.

The problem of marriage, especially for the clergy, was another headache to be conquered. As the reader may well know, it is not easy for a person to remain unmarried for his or her entire life. Unless the person is obsessed by a religious issue, it is difficult in all senses of the word to live without a companion of the opposite sex. But there are not many people in the world who are at the stage in which everything in life can be pushed aside in for the sake of one religious question. Thus, Sot'aesan concluded that it was normal for people to marry. Because training in the art of the Way does not have to be done apart from the secular world, it should be possible to continue even after getting married. The same goes for a job. Most people have to work for a living. Is this not why the Zen Buddhist maxim says "if you do not work (in the fields) for one day, do not eat that day?" Sot'aesan firmly believed that monks had been overly dependent on others for their livelihood. In his mind, true training should be able to stand alone within the busy routine of everyday life.

If so, the following counterargument could be made. How is everyday activity and training to be differentiated? However, Sot'aesan was confident in his own teachings. Because he had extracted the essence of Buddhist and Taoist teachings, he thought that training and everyday life were entirely compatible. As mentioned before, reciting the Buddha's name was for noisy places or when one was feeling nervous, and Zen meditation was to be done in opposite situations. This made it possible to train anywhere at any time. Training methods of the past required excessive sacrifice in order to reach enlightenment; I am not sure how practically minded teachings of Sot'aesan would stand muster to these. In any case, it seems that anyone who founds a new religion must be confident in oneself to survive amidst existing established religions.

Sot'aesan introduced various ways to train but he also offered lifestyles that were appropriate for the various stages of life. Above all else, young people are to study. This was the command of Sot'aesan, who was a firm believer in education. When approaching middle age, religious training begins. Sot'aesan called this 'the study of the Way.' But because one is still living in society, one cannot afford to ignore one's job. Sot'aesan believed that working in social welfare rather than in a profit-oriented business was the ideal form of work. While it was fine and good to work, if possible it should be for the good of others. In old age, one is to detach oneself from all worldly concerns and focus on training. This is very similar to the Hindu division of life into four stages: the learning stage (as a student), the family stage (working to support a family), the retirement stage (beginning of training) and the priesthood stage (leaving home to focus entirely on training). One cannot help but be amazed by the similarities between the two religions' division of life. Sot'aesan probably wanted to prove that training in this fashion would make enlightenment entirely possible within the boundaries of everyday life.

The last point related to Buddhist reform that Sot'aesan criticized was about ritual procedures. As he pointed out, traditional Buddhism had little interest in secular rituals. But in Buddhism's defense, all ceremonies and rituals during the Chosŏn dynasty were performed in Confucian style, making temples obsolete. There was no need to visit far-away temples because weddings, ancestral rites and funerals were all conducted at home. Although this may have been true a century ago, the diminished influence of Confucianism in Korea today shows that Sot'aesan was eventually right. It is to the point that Buddhist couples are married in wedding halls rather than at the temple. In comparison, Won Buddhism has a detailed collection of ceremonial rules that include almost every possible type of occasion. This includes even the exact sermon that should be given at funerals, making things much easier for the deceased person's family. There are also rules for coming-of-age ceremony, weddings, sixtieth birthday ceremony, Buddhist funeral and various other events that occur most frequently in everyday life as well as for temple festivities. At the back of the book is a section that describes what should be written on the flag for births, deaths and funeral tablets. The level of detail for each of these is astounding to say the least. It is a testament to Sot'aesan's desire to create the perfect type of everyday Buddhism as well as his confidence, meticulousness and lack of deficiency.

We have now covered all the high points of Sot'aesan's teachings. We have covered in great detail training methods, the *Il-Won* principle that becomes revealed through such training and how to create a just society, which is an expression of love for others. But there are still some points left to discuss. We will see the progress that has been made by Won Buddhism over the years. What is the use of having nothing but fancy doctrines? The most important thing is how much these doctrines have been put into practice. Won Buddhism is the new religion that has remained the most faithful to the teachings of its founder, both in terms of breadth and depth. Let us see the current state of Won Buddhism as well as ideas for its future development.

Chapter 4

Won Buddhism Today and Its Problems

Won Buddhism in the World

Won Buddhism has entered the era of its fifth Prime Dharma Master—this is the highest rank in Won Buddhism—Kyŏngsan. It is nearly impossible to list all of the organizations that are directly or indirectly affiliated with Won Buddhism because of their sheer number. There are currently 1.2 million self-professed Won Buddhists in Korea, but of course the official figure is much smaller. In terms of the number of believers, it is the fifth largest religion in Korea after Buddhism, Protestantism, Catholicism and Confucianism. Within Korea there are fifteen parishes and 450 temples, with 80 ministers in over 13 countries to spread the teachings of Won Buddhism. Among the religions that originate in Korea—except for the Unification Church—Won Buddhism is the only one that has spread all over the world. Among its overseas institutions, one of the most influential ones is in the United States: the Won Institute of Graduate Studies in Philadelphia. The dean of this university, Minister Pok In Kim, is the daughter of third Prime Dharma Master Taesan and a fellow alumna of the religion department at Temple University; thus, I know the school quite well. Because the Won Institute of Graduate Studies is officially licensed by the state of Pennsylvania, it is able to award advanced degrees and is the only school in the US that has been established by a Korean religion. The US is not known for having loose regulations on the establishment of universities. In fact, it is an extremely complicated process, but Minister Kim finally succeeded after years of pushing her agenda to the Philadelphia municipal government.

With this much effort invested in schools overseas, there is no reason to believe any differently for domestic institutions. Of course the most famous of these is Wonkwang University, which we discussed in the chapter on Chŏngsan. Having begun from a humble two-room house, nobody could have foreseen its transformation into the large elite private university that it is today. Furthermore, in Yongkwang (Sot'aesan's hometown) there is a college specializing in producing ministers; there are also ten middle and high schools. One interesting fact is that there are three Won Buddhist-run 'alternative schools' for problem students who have trouble adjusting to regular public schools. From what I hear, these alternative schools are highly successful. One recently established alternative school is for North Korean refugee teens.

In addition to schools, there are many social welfare institutions that would take up too much space to list individually here. There are close to one hundred nursing homes, orphanages, homes for the handicapped, psychiatric wards and facilities for low income families. Each of these many establishments needs a minister to be in charge, but as the pool of ministers diminishes each year it seems that the Won Buddhist order is struggling to fix the situation. Furthermore, these small independent facilities are not the only ones under Won Buddhist control. It also owns large-scale hospitals that are affiliated with its universities. There are separate hospitals that each specialize in Western medicine, Oriental medicine, psychiatrics and dentistry; there are many Oriental medicine hospitals and pharmacies in nine cities throughout Korea. In addition, there are countless profit organizations in the areas of agriculture, industry and business that seem to have originated from Sot'aesan's early business activities. This can be interpreted to mean that the accumulation of wealth through work in the secular world is just as important as religious training.

From an outsider's perspective, the most eye-catching of all Won Buddhist activity is the effort invested in dialogue between religions. This was briefly mentioned in our discussion of Chŏngsan, but one of the central tenets of Won Buddhism states that "all religions are one." This comes from one of Sot'aesan's sermons. According to Sot'aesan, all religions come from the same root: the following is the analogy that he used to describe it. A person who had a family in Korea went on a trip through several countries and had a new family in each one. Later, all of his children gathered in one place. Although they all have the same father, it was difficult for them to get along at first because they had grown up in completely different environments. But as the years passed, they began to understand one another and learned to cooperate. Sot'aesan believed that this was the current situation of all the religions in the world. Although all religions are from the same source, they became too different from each other because they were each developed in different cultural spheres. This is why there is no end to religious warfare, but this is to stop in the near future as people become more open to each other. This is obviously an optimistic interpretation on the part of Sot'aesan, but Won Buddhism is nevertheless playing a very active role in this forthcoming dialogue through international religious organizations such as the World Conference on Religion and Peace (KCRP) and the International Association for Religious Freedom (IARF). I have participated in several of these conferences, and there are always so many Won Buddhists that it gives the impression that Won Buddhism is the only form of Buddhism in Korea. The Congress of World Religions, begun in Chicago in 1893, held a special conference in commemoration of its hundredth anniversary in 1993. Of all the representatives of the world's religions, a Won Buddhist female minister named Oŭn had the honor of being included in a delegation of ten representatives, which not only was an honor for Won Buddhism but Korean women as well.

Apart from these, Won Buddhism was the first new religion to have its own TV station (Wonŭm Broadcasting) as well as hold services in military bases.[1] Thus, Won Buddhist ministers were given the same right to hold religious gatherings on military bases as Buddhist monks, Catholic priests and Protestant ministers.

We have seen a rough overview of the Won Buddhist organizational structure, but a closer look would reveal countless more affiliated organizations. Did not Sot'aesan once say that of all the religious work he did in his previous lives, this was by far the largest in scale? The Won Buddhist order is currently so large and

1 Unlike the US and most other Western European countries, military service is a mandatory duty for all healthy Korean men regardless of religious affiliation. No exception is made for those who (e.g. Buddhists) are not permitted to fight in battle under the rules of their religion.

continuously growing at such a rapid pace that Sot'aesan's conviction is entirely believable. This does not mean, however, that there are no problems within this structure. Let us go over several of the more serious ones.

Best Teaching, Rundown Infrastructure

Until now, we have only seen the bright side of Won Buddhism. But no organization is free from faults or things that need to be fixed. Thus, our discussion of Won Buddhism remains incomplete without an evaluation of its problems. The most serious problem faced by Won Buddhism today is the same one that exists for all Korean traditional religions: the problem of modernization. In short, the religion is unable to play a leading role in the current era. It is what I always tell Won Buddhists whenever I meet them: the 'content' of Won Buddhism is excellent but it is packaged terribly. Although Sot'aesan's teachings are among the best in the world, it is not being presented on the same level as the quality of its parts.

I also say the same thing in this way. Sot'aesan said that "With this Great Opening of matter, let there be a Great Opening of spirit," but I want to say that the great opening of matter has not yet occurred for Won Buddhism. The reason for this is simple. The temple-centric culture is too outdated. First of all, it is easy for there to be a uniform way of doing things because it is a single-denomination religion. But each temple looks different, all lacking Won Buddhist influence in its architecture. Thus, there is no sense that the building has been built with utmost devotion or that it is Won Buddhist. Compared to Buddhism, Won Buddhism is like a venture business. What, by definition, is 'venture?' A venture company has to have a unique set of strategies to maintain a competitive edge in the face of older and larger companies. This is the only way that it can remain competitive and survive. Then how can Won Buddhism survive? I do not yet see a unique Won Buddhist strategy; this is apparent even only by discussing its buildings. Because of the 1,600-year history of Buddhism, there are many beautiful Buddhist structures that can easily hold their own anywhere in the world. This is a huge asset, because it is often enough to attract many new believers. By contrast, the situation in Won Buddhism is very different. More than anything else, the temples are not as advanced as their Buddhist counterparts. As I said earlier, Won Buddhist temples are not very attractive. If I held an influential post within the order, I would assemble a Won Buddhist Committee on Religious Culture and recruit the best architects in Korea (and from other countries if necessary) to create a completely different type of temple structure that is also still rooted in tradition. This would then become the template by which all other temples are built. We live in a material world; thus, our material circumstances must be stable first and foremost. There is a reason why churches and temples are built with so much care.

The problem does not only lie in the outer appearance of buildings. The interior also lacks any redeeming qualities. Some temples use the same long benches that are found in churches; indeed, one need only cover the *Il-Won-Sang* at the front and the surroundings would look no different from a church. On the other hand, some temple hold services while sitting on the floor. This is also something that should be standardized.

This is not the only problem that Won Buddhism faces today. There is no real religious culture as of yet. This is obvious just from observing the order in which a Won Buddhist service is conducted, much of which reminds me of a church service. In addition, all 'hymns' are sung with piano accompaniment. I have always objected to Won Buddhist songs being played on a piano; I do not pretend to understand why songs that declare loyalty to Buddha are played on a Western instrument and sung according to Western vocal patterns. But Won Buddhists apparently see nothing wrong with this practice. I have pointed this out many times: "Let's face it: there is no way that you will catch up to the advanced level of Catholic and Protestant hymns by singing Won Buddhist and Buddhist songs in harmony patterns of western music. Why not instead focus on developing something that you do well, like reciting the Buddha's name? It is actually very difficult for people regardless of sex or age to all sing in the exact same key. Instead, we have traditional Korean methods of singing that make harmony possible even when everyone sings in his or her own pitch. That is what Korean tradition is. But why is this abandoned in favor of only Western music?" I do not know whether the lack of reaction to these views is because of a failure to understand or not wanting to understand.

Thus, I give Won Buddhists the following analogy. Won Buddhism is working so hard to become a worldwide religion. Let us suppose that an American who is interested in Won Buddhism visits a Won Buddhist temple in the US. If this American sat in on a Won Buddhist service, what would he think? He would have wanted to see a form of Buddhism that is uniquely Korean and different from its Chinese and Japanese counterparts, but not even the building gives much of an impression of Korea or even the Far East. The interior design is also awkward. Something about the service does not feel right. It is too similar to a church worship service. The songs that are sung at various intervals also sound strange. The same codes that are repeated over and over again are too simple and there is no harmony at all. It is difficult to tell whether the songs are in the Eastern or Western cultural tradition. He has come to this temple in order to feel something different from the clergy-centric doctrine and infrastructure of Christianity that he wanted to escape from, but it is a huge disappointment because everything about Won Buddhism seems to only be imitating Christian aspects. This is basically the impression I imagine a non-Korean would receive. Minister Pok In Kim, who is currently proselytizing in the United States, says that there are almost no Westerners at the weekly service.

The same situation is true within Korea. Any religion that wants to grow needs to attract young people. What about Won Buddhism would be attractive to young people in their teens and twenties? The outside world has entered the twenty-first century, but stepping inside the temple is like traveling back in time to the seventies and eighties. Buddhist buildings were built in late Chosŏn, which gives them an authentic aura, but this same feeling is nonexistent for Won Buddhist buildings. The sequence of services would look too old-fashioned for younger people. Also, the scriptural teachings are too polished and dignified. This is the general impression that I believe a young person would receive of Won Buddhism today. Predictably, there is always a shortage of young Won Buddhists. At Ewha Womans University (the oldest women's university in Korea and the largest of its kind in the world) where I teach, most of the Won Buddhist students I know are in the religion because their parents are Won Buddhists; there are almost no believers who have entered on their own accord. This means that evangelism has completely failed. If this trend continues, Won Buddhism will end up only being passed down in the family with no new converts. When I point these things out to Won Buddhists, most of them agree with me but display no further reaction. Thus, I always say something like this: "If Won Buddhism wishes to remain a minority religion, go right ahead. The order will never grow in this way. But is this not a pity? Would it not be a shame if Won Buddhism were to remain eternally at the sidelines and never have a chance to stand at the center of Korean society? In fact, Sot'aesan's teachings would raise Korea's reputation if they were to be spread throughout the world. As a Korean myself, I cannot help but feel sorry for this state of affairs."

Then, why has the situation been left to deteriorate in this way? Why are these wonderful teachings not allowed to come out into the open? This book is neither the place nor is it within my ability to provide a comprehensive analysis of Won Buddhism. The biggest problem in Won Buddhism is most likely the fact that it is an aged religion. As I mentioned before, the venture business is too full of old people to be able to rise up. Young Won Buddhist ministers say that their opinions almost never make it up the hierarchy to those in power. This practice needs to be stopped immediately. While the wisdom of the elderly is an important asset, older leaders have difficulty adjusting to the demands of a constantly changing world. In this case, older people should simply build the fence inside which young people can grow and step down from the frontlines of leadership. This is the only way that everyone can survive together. A good organization is one that is able to constantly 'step lively;' even if left on its own it will be a living and breathing organization. This is what is currently lacking in Won Buddhism.

Another problem is that central headquarters is located far

from Seoul. Korea has followed a strange course of development that only focused on the capital city. Everything important is in Seoul, and the difference between it and the outlying provincial areas is too great. In the outer provinces, it is nearly impossible to have a feel for how the world is changing. Much as I dislike this situation, reality cannot be avoided. Then, the main administrative office needs to be in Seoul. In this way, the religion can always react swiftly and flexibly to the changing times. As a rule, a religion must always be ahead of its time in order to survive; if not, it is only a burden on society. On top of this, Koreans tend to underestimate their own culture. When I expressed my intention to write a book on the five great teachers up to Chŏngsan, the most common reaction was "why would a saint come from Korea." The reasoning is that enlightened teachers would only come from the West or perhaps India; how could a spiritual teacher possibly emerge from such an obscure place (like Korea)? There are also professors of Confucianism and Buddhism who, without having ever read Won Buddhist or Chŭngsangyo's scripture, argue that these ideologies do not stand up to the test of scholarship. This is religious elitism. I worry whether Won Buddhism will be able to overcome these varied social prejudices.

Others have an entirely different kind of concern. These people argue that Won Buddhism cannot succeed because its teachings are too rational. What is meant is that Won Buddhism does not have popular support because it does not cater to the desire of the masses, for whom religion is something that grants them what they pray for. In addition to what we have discussed in this chapter, there are many other problems faced by Won Buddhism today. I will not expound on these here because this book is an introduction to Won Buddhism for the general reader and not a proposal of solutions for the Won Buddhist leadership. I can only ask the reader to try reading Won Buddhist scripture. There will be more jewels of wisdom to be found than this book could cover.

Appendix:

More teachings of Sot'aesan not to miss

This section is a revised version of what was published in my previous book *People of the Great Awakening Period.* In this book I summarized the teachings of five teachers who represent Korea (including Sot'aesan and Chŏngsan). I wrote it in the belief that they can shed a ray of light on a spiritually starved Korea. Here I discuss select teachings of Sot'aesan and Chŏngsan that are still relevant today.

Korea: Spiritual Leader of the World

Korea's teachers had an optimistic outlook for the future of the country. Sot'aesan and Chŏngsan were no exception, but they predicted Korea's future in far greater detail than their predecessors. According to Sot'aesan, the Korea of his day was simply at the first stage of its eventual rise to greatness. More specifically, Korea would be fortunate enough to transform into a powerful nation in the same way that a fish transforms into a dragon. While this may not sound special today, it was a truly amazing prophesy considering the state of the country while Sot'aesan was alive. As

I have mentioned numerous times in this book, Korea at the time was a Japanese colony and thus the name 'Korea' was not to be found on any map. Furthermore, no one knew how long the oppressive rule of the Japanese would continue. People may very well have believed that things would eternally remain this way. The words of a famous Korean poet are brought to mind. Repenting of his past as a Japanese sympathizer, he said that he thought the Japanese empire would last for at least a century. Many collaborators probably believed the same thing. They most likely defected to the Japanese side because they did not think the Korean nation would rise again; otherwise, there is no way that so many prominent Koreans would have become collaborators. An Changho faced a similar dilemma. Although he was one of the few leaders who did not become a Japanese sympathizer, he does not seem to have been completely confident in Korean independence either. His last words on his deathbed were "Do not despair." This sounds more like a passive acceptance of fate than hope for the future.

Amidst all of this, Sot'aesan was confident. He said that Korea would not only develop but that "from a spiritual perspective, our nation will become the leader of many nations of this world. Nowadays Korea is gradually going through the process of 'a fish turning into a dragon.'" Amazingly, half of this prophesy has come true. The transformation from a per capita GDP of $58 in 1953 to approximately $20,000 in 2011 is a level of growth that has yet to be imitated by any other nation in the world. In addition, Korea is always ranked twelfth or thirteenth in trade, first or second in semiconductor production, IT powerhouse, fifth or sixth in automobile production, the best in shipbuilding and the best in digital television technology, among other things. Korea is no longer a country that was erased from the map but a leading nation. No one ever thought that Korea would develop to this extent. In fact, there were many who looked at Korea after the Korean War and declared that they would "be damned if South Korea rises up from this." But Korea did rise up. Is this not a fish turned into a dragon?

But Sot'aesan's other prediction, that Korea would be a spiritual leader of the world, does not show any indication of coming true. His disciple Chŏngsan agreed on this point; he went one step further and argued that "our nation is a leading nation in the spirit and the parent of all religions." Thus, any country that invades Korea would never succeed. Chŏngsan also predicted that Koreans would no longer be ashamed of having been born Korean but would become proud of their origins. While Korea may be weak and have nothing to offer the world now, it would eventually become a moral leader among nations. It was even said that the reunification of Korea would bring an end to war in the world. It would be wonderful if all of these things were really to come true, but the prediction that Korea will be a moral leader seems far-off. Rather, it seems to be a goal that Korea can follow for the future. While powerful nations cannot be morally superior because of the many bad things they have done, Korea was always under the subjugation of other countries and thus has nothing to be ashamed of in this regard. In these terms, I wonder whether Korea may not be able to be a guide or friend of developing countries. Another reason why these two teachers could argue these things is that they were confident in the truth of their teachings. They believed that their teachings could be the foundation of a morally superior nation that dominated the world.

On this point, Sot'aesan predicted that Korea would come to light through Hangeul (Korean Language) and the Diamond

Mountains. When a disciple expounded on the importance of scriptures written in Chinese, Sot'aesan advised that a scripture needs to be in a language that all people can understand. He even predicted that the day would come in which people all over the world would translate Korean scriptures into their own languages. Not all of this has come true yet, but it seems to be an expression of Sot'aesan's confidence in his work. The same is true of the Diamond Mountains. He predicted that the Diamond Mountains, a treasure of Korea, would raise Korea's standing in the international community (the same is true of the opposite). The fate of Korea and the Diamond Mountains are as one, becoming the light of the world. There has been considerable discussion on the greatness of these mountains, which makes Sot'aesan's prophesy believable. But not a lot is known about the Diamond Mountains, and thus it is difficult to evaluate them at the moment. In any case, there is no doubt that reading Sot'aesan and Chŏngsan's teachings allow Koreans to feel good about themselves.

On Death and Dying

Almost all of Sot'aesan's teachings are designed to be easily understood. There are no castles in the air; everything can be directly applied to everyday life. The same is true of his attitude on death. Sot'aesan put it in very simple terms. Human beings go through the cycle of reincarnation; for us, life and death are like two sides of the same coin and are thus the cornerstone of existence. Most people are only interested in how to live and do not realize that death is just as important. Within the context of reincarnation, only a good death can guarantee being born into a favorable status in the next life. Birth, in turn, determines the quality of that life. However, most people spend far too little time preparing for death. Sot'aesan believed that one should begin preparing to die after the age of forty.

When a disciple asked him what happens after death, Sot'aesan answered according to the traditional Buddhist worldview. After leaving the body, the spirit enters a spirit world—called the 'middle world' in Buddhist terminology—and wanders around until it receives the body it will inhabit in the next life. In some cases, the next body is received right after death. But in the vast majority of cases, the spirit does not realize that it has died and roams about, believing that it still has its old body. It then receives a new body when it has reached the place that it is to live. The concept of reincarnation is a complex one and is a discussion for an entirely different book. But as intellectual capacity grows larger (especially in the twenty-first century), reincarnation theory is receiving increasing support from scholars as well as those who consider themselves religious. It is especially popular among Western academics for the following reason. While we cannot know about reincarnation in a normal state of mind, this information is easily accessible once we go deeper into the inner consciousness. Therefore, from a rational point of view, it is considered naïve to rule out the possibility of reincarnation.

During Chŏngsan's tenure as Prime Dharma Master, a disciple who had received a Western education of sorts denied the reincarnation theory. Chŏngsan immediately retorted that one should not discount the teachings of great teachers of the past with such shallow knowledge. According to Chŏngsan, the only way to have a legitimate opinion of *karma* or reincarnation was to remain silent and in an enlightened state of mind for three months. Only after reflecting one's mind on truth would it be possible to truly understand the nature of *karma*. Thus, to Chŏngsan it was not a subject to be discussed carelessly.

Even more interesting than Sot'aesan's philosophy on death is his philosophy on how to die (called 'well-dying' in today's context). Even here we can feel his greatness as a teacher. Dying is extremely important for all people to the point that the mark of a life well lived is a peaceful death. At the same time, because it is such a frightening experience for obvious reasons, people do their best to avoid it for as long as possible. Then, one suddenly dies as if whisked away by the angel of death to a place that no living person can ever go. This fear of death and dying is especially prevalent among Koreans, who have long been influenced by Confucian culture. Confucianism does not have a concept of anything outside of this life and is thus firmly rooted in the goal to continue life as long as humanly possible. This is why there are so many unfortunate scenes in the intensive care units of Korean hospitals. Even when the patient knows that the cancer is beyond treatment, he continues to insist on chemotherapy. The patient's family that has to give him round-the-clock care is taxed to the end of their strength physically, emotionally and financially. Thus, the patient dies after a great deal of unnecessary pain and the family is left with astronomical hospital bills that are beyond their ability to pay. It is a situation in which no one benefits. All of this continues to happen because Koreans do not have a definite idea about death. Sot'aesan's lessons on death and dying can be of considerable help in this sense.

Sot'aesan, ever the meticulous leader, had a highly pragmatic approach to educating people about dying. The pragmatism indicates that not only the person about to die but his family is presented with a detailed agenda on how to prepare for the death of a loved one. There is probably no other religious leader who presented a template this considerate about death. The first thing that is listed is what the dying person himself has to do. When a person feels that he will die soon, he is to begin wrapping up all his activities and think about concluding his life. The will is also to be written at this stage so that it need not be worried about later. As the hour of death approaches, the most important thing is to achieve mental unity. If the person has committed grievances against others or if there are uncollected favors still lying around, he should call the individual in question to his bed and settle each issue face-to-face. If this is not possible, the issue must be resolved within one's own heart. The last thought of a person is very important in Buddhism because this has great influence over what he or she will be reborn as in the next life. Even if one has done many bad things in the previous life, true repentance just before death can bring a better life in the next world. When a person who had done many bad deeds in the previous life was reborn into a good life, an investigation of the matter revealed that the individual had repented just before he died. In this sense, Sot'aesan's ideas are a continuation of Buddhist practices.

The next most important thing to do is to completely let go of carnal lust or greed. If this is not done, one undergoes a difficult death and spends a lot of time wandering around afterwards. After having made such efforts, one must meet death while chanting Buddha's name or meditating in order to leave this life with a clean mind. Education about dying is so beneficial that even people who were never interested in death can have good results. However, the problem is that preparation cannot be crammed into the short period just before death; it must be done over an extended period of time. As mentioned previously, one needs to begin thinking about death from the age of forty. The most important thing here is to release the grudges of the heart and the desire to cling to life. Most of us, of course, fail to follow the latter.

A person about to die desperately needs the help of those close to him in order to overcome his obsession with living. This is because death cannot be peaceful if his friends and family are always busy fighting amongst themselves. Won Buddhism had the concept of a Buddhist hospice long before its western counterpart entered Korea. The first thing for the family to do is to light incense sticks so that the patient can maintain inner calm. Under the same logic, the room (or house) is kept quiet with no loud noises. Conversation with the patient should only be about good things so that his benevolent tendencies will be awakened and his mind put at rest. Immoral or lascivious talk can remain in his heart and be taken with him into the next life. The thing that should be avoided the most is worrying about the rest of the family and other issues like inheritance within earshot of the patient. This causes the dying person to attach himself to the material aspects of the life that will soon end. It is helpful to recite Buddha's name or read scriptures to the patient for the sake of his mental and spiritual stability. But if the patient does not want this, it is fine to simply sit in silence.

The most important point is the last one. Even if the patient is about to die and is gasping for breath, no one is to weep aloud, call out to him or shake him. Such intense demonstrations only disturb a person who is about to leave this world and have no positive effect. Sot'aesan strongly advises that if one cannot help but weep, it should be done several hours after his spirit has left for good. This type of teaching is not found in any other religion. This piece of advice may be useless to those who believe that death is the end of everything, but it is extremely important for those who believe in the concept of reincarnation and a new life after death. When one's parents have passed away, most Koreans will sob loudly and make a commotion almost as wild as having a fit. It is impossible to avoid this because in Confucianism, making a huge display of grief is indicative of filial piety. However, Sot'aesan firmly presses the brakes against this practice.

The following anecdote appears in *Life After Life*, a seminal work on near-death experience by Raymond Moody Jr. A person came back to life after she had died. Upon returning to her senses, she requested that no prayers be said the next time she died. The reason for this was that her family's prayers held back her spirit as it tried to leave the body, preventing it from flying free. Sot'aesan had the same opinion, but his teaching is even more compassionate because it does not forget to consider the dead person's family. Not preventing weeping altogether but permitting it after several hours have passed is a measure that is practical while at the same time embraces the grief of those left behind.

The Lesson of Karma

For Sot'aesan, who believed in reincarnation, cause and effect theory was common sense. Indeed, there is a saying in Buddhism that "if you want to know about your previous life, look at the hardships of your current life; if you want to know about your future life, look at what you are doing now." Sot'aesan had several things to say about this doctrine, which I will summarize below.

One female believer whose relationship with her husband had soured, vowing to have nothing to do with him in her next life. Sot'aesan advised the following: "If you want to avoid creating any further affinities with your husband, don't entertain either a detesting or a loving mind, but treat him only with no-mind. If you do not do so and choose to either detest him or love him, this will leave a possibility for you to be brought together again in the next life." This teaching reveals several points. Buddhist teaching states that one should create neither loved ones nor enemies because all relationships are formed through the invisible strength of accumulated *karma*. Things are not too different today, but this was even more true in the past. The story of the itinerant husband who dies suddenly from alcohol abuse is common gossip in Korea. According to psychoanalysts, the typical Korean male becomes a mama's boy because of the traditional Confucian practice of son-preference that permeates most families. As a result, this creates many negative complexes about the mother, who lives vicariously through her son and is a constantly hovering presence in his life. This psychological burden—the knowledge of having been exploited by one's mother—is then transferred to the wife in the form of abuse. Sot'aesan's female disciple in the anecdote seems to have suffered this exact phenomenon. While it is easy to talk about not having hateful feelings towards such a husband, it is extremely difficult to put into practice. Because it is so difficult, most people continue to create *karma* and suffer its consequences. This is the Buddhist interpretation.

Many Buddhists are interested in which acts cause which types of consequences. Sot'aesan explains the answer to this with a simple example, which I introduce here because it will be helpful to those who believe in cause and effect theory. If a person makes many careless comments that hurt others' feelings, he will suffer great heartache in his next life. Also, a person who enjoys listening on others' secrets will be born illegitimate in his next life and endure a lifetime of ridicule. A person who likes to reveal others' secrets and embarrass people in public will have a large mole or scar on his face in his next life, making it impossible for him to live normally in society. Ordinary people like us cannot know whether these predictions about the three lifetimes are true or not. Furthermore, this teaching is so simplified that it may bring about a lot of undesirable side effects. Buddha is famous for having not discussed this type of transgenerational reincarnation that exceeds human ability to control. This was probably because of the potential for its abuse.

However, a similar story was told on the other side of the world. Edgar Casey, the most famous American prophet of the twentieth century, made a claim very similar to that of Sot'aesan, despite being Christian rather than Buddhist. Casey was famous for prescribing medication for sick people in the state of self-hypnosis. One day, while he was under deep hypnosis, he realized that people live multiple lives. Casey was initially taken aback by the discovery of a truth that does not agree with Christian doctrine and debated it for awhile, but eventually overcame his doubts. The rest of the story is far too long and complicated to tell here, but the fact that this American Christian reached the same conclusion as Sot'aesan is worth noting.

The following example is one of the Casey's explanations of *karma*. Casey tried to cure one woman who suffered from severe obesity with medication, but it did not work very well. At his wit's end, he examined her past life and found that she had ridiculed someone for being fat. It was only after she truly repented of her wrongdoing that she was cured of obesity. Another person was born deaf; an examination of his previous life revealed that when someone in desperate need asked him for help, he pretended to not be able to hear. As a result, he was born deaf in his next life. As such, *karma* basically means being born with the opposite result of something from the previous life that can be fixed upon repenting and seeking forgiveness. Readers who are not accustomed to the idea of multiple lives may think this sounds absurd. However, it does not seem right to ignore the conclusion that various religious teachers have reached who are far more in tune spiritually than we are. As Jesus once said, "He who has ears to hear, let him hear (NIV, Luke 14:35)."

Sot'aesan told another interesting story about what it is like in hell. Religious teachers do not describe things in a complicated manner. They make use of examples easily found in everyday life to make their explanations more entertaining and easy to understand. One day, a disciple was in the kitchen chopping meat. Sot'aesan asked this disciple whether he had seen "Sword Mountain Hell." Sword Mountain Hell is one of the various hells that exist in folk Buddhism, a place riddled with knives as far as the eye can see and where the unfortunate person is confined to be cut by the knives for eternity. Sot'aesan's ever-insightful observation follows: "The meat on the cutting board is in Sword Mountain Hell. When it was being killed, it was hacked by meat axes and sliced by knives into thousands of pieces. Then, several people buy these cuts of meat and again cut them in their homes with thousand knives. How could this not be terrifying?" This is not an easy observation to make. It is impossible to be able to explain the mundane events of everyday life in such a way without being deeply enlightened. Of course, Sot'aesan did not mean that everyone should blindly believe in Sword Mountain Hell. He knew that the idea itself was a metaphor to be used for better understanding of Buddhist principles. The pain suffered in this hell can be interpreted to mean psychological pain; the feeling of having one's heart ripped into a million pieces is something that even regular people can relate to. Explaining this with an everyday concept like cutting meat ensures that even the most simple- minded can understand the point. Most of all, people who have heard this story will do their best to not hurt others, which is the real purpose of the entire exercise. Sot'aesan's method of tailoring his messages to match the intellectual level of his audience was amazingly fine tuned.

Creating the Ideal Family

There are many more teachings of Sot'aesan; covering them all would require at least several more books. But there is one last point that I would like to share with the reader: the way to maintain the ideal family and the corresponding method of proper education of children. Because the family is the foundation of society, in a sense it is obvious that the family must be stable for society to be stable. Thus, while it is expected that a religious leader would discuss the family, no religion as of yet has provided rules or guidance on this matter. Sot'aesan exceeds other religious founders in this aspect as well. What were his teachings about the ideal family?

The formation of an ideal family is explained with nine categories, which we need not examine one by one here. The head of the family is responsible for teaching the rest of the family, but he or she must first be learned himself or herself and be a mirror for the family to be reflected upon. The head of the family must not be engaged in a profession that kills living things or inflict pain on other people. There must also of course be financial independence in married couples for the achievement of a wealthy and prosperous society. In addition to one's duties as a citizen, one must always be prepared to provide assistance to welfare institutions. Sot'aesan always emphasized the public good especially when related to the education of one's children. He argues that children should be educated in both the sciences and religion; after this education is complete, they should spend a significant amount of time engaged in some form of community service. His logical turn of mind can be seen on the issue of property inheritance as well. Sot'aesan does not forbid the passing down of property or wealth to one's children but states that only just enough to begin a nest egg should be provided, with the rest given as a donation to society. It is a reaffirmation or Sot'aesan's public-minded philosophy. A society made up of this type of family is a wonderful place to imagine, but in reality such a family is a rare sight; most families are only concerned with their own children.

In relation to this, Sot'aesan also subdivides the proper education of one's children into various categories. It can be understood as the following four concepts: teaching with the heart, teaching by action, teaching with words and teaching in a strict manner. These are sometimes divided into nine categories instead of four. One must first be obedient to one's own parents in order to avoid being a hypocrite before one's children. One's words and actions must be authoritative but at the same time affection must not be neglected. This is because without the love of compassion, children cannot be moved to act. Also, promises made to children must always be kept so that credit is not lost. There are many parents even today who are not good at keeping promises with their children. This was probably even more prevalent back then when the rights of offspring were not even taken into consideration. Reward and punishment are also to be appropriately administered. Sot'aesan did not fail to incorporate religion and public spirit; in order to stand firm in the face of worldly temptations, strong religious faith must be taught along with a sense of public spirit. Children who are raised in this way would no doubt grow up to be fine adults; the person who put this into action the best is Sot'aesan himself. He raised all of his children to be exemplary people in a method beyond reproach.

저자: 최준식
(사) 한국문화표현단 이사장
한국죽음학회장
이화여자대학교 국제대학원 한국학과 교수
이화여자대학교 한국문화연구원장

저서
『한국의 종교, 문화로 읽는다』 1, 2, 3
『종교를 넘어선 종교』
『무교, 권력에서 밀린 한국인의 근본신앙』
『최준식의 한국종교사 바로보기』
The development of "three-religions-are-one" principle from China to Korea 외

원불교: 한국 불교의 탄생　　값 18,000원

2011년 9월 5일 1판 1쇄

저　　자　최 준 식
발 행 인　임 삼 규
발 행 처　**지 문 당**
주　　소　413-756 경기도 파주시 교하읍 문발리 514-7(본사)
　　　　　110-360 서울시 종로구 와룡동 95번지(서울사무소)
등　　록　1997. 12. 30. 제406-2003-000038호
영 업 부　(02)743-3192~3　팩스(02)742-4657
전자우편　sale@jimoon.co.kr
편 집 부　(02)743-3096　팩스(02)743-0227
전자우편　edit@jimoon.co.kr
홈페이지　www.jimoon.co.kr

ISBN 978-89-6297-035-7